Writing Handbooks

Writing for a Living

Michael Legat

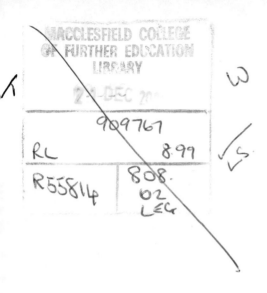
First published 2000

A & C Black (Publishers) Limited
35 Bedford Row, London WC1R 4JH

ISBN 0–7136–5398–1

A CIP catalogue record for this book
is available from the British Library.

Typeset in 10½ on 12 pt Sabon
Printed and bound in Great Britain by
Creative Print and Design (Wales), Ebbw Vale

Contents

1. Writing for a Living?

Financial prospects

If you are thinking of becoming a writer, it might be good sense to stop before you do anything else and ask yourself why. Perhaps it isn't a question of becoming a writer – you have always written, but are now taking the idea a little more seriously. Well, that's fine. So it is if you want to write because you have something to say – a story to tell, a message to put across, information to pass on, a record for yourself and your family – or if you simply want to do something creative with words, something through which you will express yourself. Perhaps you have a number of reasons. But if your answer, or part of it, is 'to make money', then it is time to think again.

If you are reading this book as an unpublished writer, or even as one who has got a foot on the first rung, and are dreaming not only of being regularly published, but also of the wealth which your writing will bring you, you may want to ask what the harm is in that. After all, there are stories almost every day about authors whose books have sold to publishers and book-clubs and film and television producers in countries all over the world, earning millions of dollars for the writer. And if it can happen to them, why not to you? You could then give up your boring job and live a life of comparative leisure, knocking off a new book or play or whatever it might be every now and then, enjoying all the luxury that your money will bring.

If anything like that is in your mind – well, it's a free country and you can follow your star wherever it leads, and, if you're determined enough, you have a real chance of success. But before you throw up your job, I would suggest that it's not only time to think again, it's Facing Facts Time. Writing is almost never a quick or easy way to get rich. Admittedly, every now and then an unknown writer hits the jackpot, usually with a popular novel which publishers and film producers immediately recognise as having the qualities of a potential bestseller. Such an author can give up any other employment straight away, not only because of the huge sum the book has earned, but because there is a reasonable chance of its successors doing well too. Other authors, in whatever genre they may work, may become extremely successful, but only after many years in which they earn no more than a modest income from writing, while building their reputation (Catherine Cookson is a case in point). For many thousands of published writers the longed-for renown and wealth never ever come, and their earnings from writing may not bring in more than a couple of thousand pounds a year – if that.

One of the problems is that most would-be writers think in terms of fiction. While it is true that several thousand new novels are published in this country every year, a very high proportion of them consists of books by writers who have been published before, and although publishers are always on the look-out for new talent (and remember that established writers die, or give up writing, or go out of fashion, and have to be replaced), the market for first novels is a very limited one, and a very difficult one to break into. Even if your book is unusual enough to be accepted, it may easily sink without trace when it comes out, despite the publisher's enthusiasm, and it is salutary to realise that sales of most novels have ceased within a few weeks of publication.

The market for non-fiction is much more encouraging, provided that you have something new to say about your subject, and the sales of a non-fiction work tend to go on for very much longer than those of a novel. However, even if your book becomes a standard work on its subject and continues to sell steadily year after year, in many cases the annual sale will not rise much above a few hundred, and that won't make you rich.

The message is therefore clear: do not pitch your expectations too high – indeed, it is better not to allow yourself any expectations at all – and don't even think about giving up the job which provides you with your living in favour of a writing career unless you have an adequate private income or have established yourself to such an extent that you can be sure that your earnings from what you write can be depended on and will be sufficient for your needs. This is very possibly the best bit of advice on any aspect of writing that you can ever be given. Take it to heart and remember it, especially when you have signed your first contract and are tempted to give up your present occupation in order to become a professional author. It's fine if that first contract is going to guarantee you something of the order of £50,000 and you are already being asked enthusiastically about your next project, but otherwise you will be a lot happier if you can persuade yourself to look upon what you earn from writing simply as a little pin-money. It is worth remembering, too, all the benefits which you give up if you leave your job – not only a regular wage or salary packet, but the equally regular payment of Income Tax through PAYE, which means that you do not suddenly have to find a large sum to meet the Inland Revenue's demands, plus the employer's National Insurance contributions, paid holidays, paid sick leave, etc., etc. – and in their place you will be putting an erratic, unreliable income, and will be personally responsible for all your expenses, including National Insurance and Income Tax.

It is a salutary exercise to work out a budget for yourself, listing all the expenses that will have to be met just to keep you, and anyone for whom you are responsible, alive. Forget the image of the writer starving in a garret, staying in bed for the warmth of the bedclothes, and producing a masterpiece – it's very difficult indeed to work well if you're cold and hungry. Set against your outgoings your realistic appraisal of what your writing is likely to earn for you. The answer is likely to be depressing.

After all the gloom and doom in the paragraphs above, you may feel tempted to forget about writing and to express your creative urges in some other way. Don't do that. If you believe you're a writer, nothing else will give you as much satisfaction as writing, and all you need to do is to heed the advice to keep your feet on the ground. There is no reason why you shouldn't earn a few pennies from writing, and maybe even graduate into the big time. But let that come as a pleasant surprise, rather than counting on it.

I should, however, mention Copy Writing – one form of writing which does provide a more dependable income if you are proficient at it. Diana Wimbs tells you how to set about it in *Freelance Copywriting* (published by A & C Black).

When and where to work

1 Writing regularly
If you talk to professional writers, they will all tell you the same thing – that writing is a job like any other. If you want to look upon it simply as a hobby, which you can busy yourself with or

leave alone as the mood takes you, that's your choice, but, unless you are a genius (which very few of us are), you are not likely to get very far. The difference between the attitude of the professional, who sees writing as a job to be done, and that of the dilettante amateur, is often the difference between success and failure. If you want to write for a living, you must be serious about when and where to work.

Many would-be writers believe that publishable material comes into being without preparation, without long and arduous labour, without any kind of revision in a search for near-perfection, and that all these requirements can be ignored, provided that the writer possesses Talent. Yet because these aspiring authors accept in the secrecy of their souls that they don't have a big enough talent, they seek for a Magic Key in books about writing. It is never there, because the key does not live in books, but is to be found within the writers themselves. The books can be immensely helpful in more practical ways, and the advice which they give may set you on the path to find the key within yourself, but your search will be in vain unless you have a capacity for hard and continuing work over a long period. Of course, some talent is indeed necessary, but only a genius has Talent with a capital T, and almost all of us have to make do with the variety which comes with a small t. You might also remember that familiar saying, 'Genius is one per cent inspiration, and ninety-nine per cent perspiration' – even a genius can rarely get by without a lot of hard work.

Stories are told, of course, of writers who, given a deadline, refuse to touch a pen or the keyboard until the last minute, or even until the material is overdue, and then rattle it off. Well, I believe such writers are fewer and farther between than they would like to believe, and in any case many of them do work on whatever it may be during the whole period preceding the dead-line, without being aware that they are doing so, because their mysterious subconscious minds are beavering away at the job.

There are many reasons why regular writing should be the rule. First of all, it is the way to get things done – if you write regularly you are likely to finish that novel or play or whatever it may be that much sooner and, as the pages pile up, you are far less likely to feel discouraged. Secondly, it is surprising how much more readily the words flow if you write every day. And thirdly, it isn't only the words which come more easily, but the ideas too.

Naturally, there will be days when you cannot write – you may be ill or too tired or caught up in events which give you no time to yourself at all, or you may allow yourself a holiday. There is nothing wrong with any of that, but you will probably find that when you return to writing, it will not be quite as easy until you get back into the swing of it. Charles Dickens said: 'If I miss writing for one day it takes me a week to get going again,' which was undoubtedly an exaggeration, but true in principle.

It is often helpful to decide on the number of words to achieve in a week, writing on as many days as possible and allowing a little latitude for the days when for some reason you cannot write. No rules can be laid down – writers work at very different rates, some contenting themselves with a couple of short paragraphs in a day and others producing several thousand words in a single session – and you just have to work out what is reasonable for you. Then give yourself a target which is a little above your expectations, and try to achieve it. Setting a target really does help you to keep your nose to the grindstone.

If you have any choice in the matter, find out at which time of day you feel happiest to write. Again, professionals vary greatly, some working best when the rest of the world is asleep and it is quiet, others writing in the morning only, or in the morning and again in the evening. If the subject ever comes up when authors get together, they are usually fascinated by what their fellow writers tell them, simply because so many different patterns are followed. You will soon find out what time of day suits you and for how long a period you can work.

But do make it a regular session, writing every day if possible, even if that means some sacrifice of your other activities.

2 Where to write

For some people the idea of having an office or even a work-space in the home is an impossible dream, and they have to do their writing in the bedroom, or in the family living-room, with the television on and the general hubbub of family life doing its best to distract them. If you can possibly manage it, however, arrange for yourself somewhere to write.

The ideal is to have a study, devoted solely to your work, to which you can escape without fear of being interrupted, and with room to spread all that you need around you. But that, of course, implies a house of reasonable size, with a room which can be spared in that way. Next best, perhaps, is a desk in your bedroom; it may be cramped, but at least you are more likely to be able to get a bit of peace and quiet there. If you live in a bedsit, or are otherwise restricted, you may need earplugs and a great deal of determination, and you will probably also find it essential, however much against the grain it may be, to be tidy – mind you, the temptation to be untidy is one of the worst aspects of having plenty of room in which to write. If your working surroundings are far from ideal, always remember that many of the great writers of the past have worked in the most difficult circumstances.

In the end, a writer can write anywhere. Some work on the train, some in the kitchen, some lying on a chaise longue, some in theatre dressing rooms, some in the various hotels where they spend weekday nights – anywhere. William Horwood has an office, away from his family home, to which he goes every day, just like any other office worker. Emulate him if that is what you want and you can afford it, or choose whatever other alternative is possible and suits you, or simply write wherever you are.

If you have any choice and the space, there are several essentials for your workroom. You will need a chair which is sufficiently comfortable (but not to such an extent that you tend to fall asleep), of the right height, and with good back support – an office chair of the swivel variety is a good bet – and a desk or table, again of the right height, to carry your p.c. and its bits and pieces, which can take up quite a lot of space, or your word processor or typewriter or writing pad, and you will also need some space for paper, stationery of other kinds, typescripts, and the like, and perhaps a shelf for reference books. A filing cabinet will be invaluable, provided that you can train yourself to use it. If you use a computer and therefore work on a screen, make sure that you are looking at it from a suitable distance – it should not be too close – and it is worth trying to place it so that when you look away from it you can see out of a window or at least some distance, because refocusing will help to obviate eyestrain. Needless to say, your chosen room should be well ventilated and neither too hot in summer nor too cold in winter.

If you can find a permanent place to establish yourself, it will mean that you don't have to clear everything up each time you stop writing, and it will undoubtedly help you in your efforts to work regularly. Do your own dusting and cleaning, by the way, unless you can trust whoever would do it otherwise not to 'tidy things up'.

Writing is an occupation with its own health hazards. Many authors are afflicted by eyestrain or backache and, although writer's cramp may not be as prevalent as it was in the days of the dip-pen, constant use of the keyboard of a computer or word processor can cause similar problems with the tendons of the arm and hand and fingers. Most such physical difficulties can be obviated or at least lessened by taking frequent breaks. Fortunately most of us need to stop and think every now and then, and this is a good opportunity to close the eyes briefly, to stretch, to flex the muscles of the hands and arms, and to walk round the room. Perhaps the biggest problem of all is that writing is mainly a sedentary occupation, so it is essential, if you are a full-time author, to take a certain amount of regular exercise. There is nothing like a long walk two or three times a week for keeping you in reasonable physical shape, and you may also find that it allows you and your subconscious an opportunity to come up with fresh ideas about whatever you are writing.

2. Setting Up as a Writer – and the Cost

Equipment

1 Typewriters, word processors and computers

The basic day-to-day costs for a writer are not excessive – it is very easy to spend far more on plants and fertilisers if you are keen gardener. However, just as a gardener will have to invest initially in a set of tools, so the writer will probably need to acquire some capital equipment, which may indeed be more expensive than the gardener's.

Handwritten material, or copy, is not acceptable nowadays, so you will have to get a typewriter or a word processor or a computer, and teach yourself to type, if you cannot do so already. All such machines use a standard qwertyuiop keyboard (which is to say that the letters are always arranged in the same order). Of course, you may be one of those writers who are anti-machine, and prefer to work in longhand, in which case the only equipment you will need is a number of pens or pencils and any kind of paper which suits you; but you will then have to pay a professional typist (unless you have a willing friend) to produce a typescript from your manuscript, and that can be expensive.

What sort of typewriter or word processor or computer should you buy, and what is it likely to cost?

The only thing that can be said nowadays in favour of buying a typewriter is that it is comparatively cheap – working on it is a slow and laborious process; mistakes are not easily corrected, and it takes a great deal of care, or much expertise, to produce error-free copy; and it is usually impossible to make more than two or three legible copies without having to retype the whole thing from the beginning. You will have to count the number of words yourself.

Word-counting and spellcheck facilities on a machine can be very useful, and are standard nowadays in virtually all word processors and personal computers. The former counts the number of words in a document with accuracy, but it makes no allowances for short lines or short pages, which publishers need to do when calculating the extent of a book. As for the spellcheck, even if you are an absolute wiz at spelling, it will usually pick up most of your typing errors, which is very helpful.

A word processor may be exactly what a writer needs. For about £200 (2000 prices), you can get a machine with a screen, on which what you type will be displayed, and with a built-in printer. Corrections are simple, printing extra copies is a matter of pushing a few buttons, and you will have a choice of fonts (typefaces) and typesizes, the ability to produce spreadsheets, and you may even have a computer game or two incorporated.

As well as your writing as an author, which may involve several different projects, you will be able to keep your accounts and records on the word processor, use it for all your correspondence, etc., and it is ideal for the purpose of running a local society or, indeed, any kind of organisation. All your material can be stored within the machine on its internal hard disc, and additionally on floppy discs (which are only floppy inside – outwardly they appear like squares of hard plastic). Floppies can be used to send your material to someone else – a publisher, for instance – or as a back-up, but although they are normally adequate for the storage of a book of 50,000 words or so, they are limited in capacity, and you would probably need a new disc for each main subject, such as different writing projects, correspondence, accounts and so on. If you write a vast saga you may need several discs in order to store it, but that is no problem.

For a cost in the region of £1000 you can buy a far more impressive package where the computer will be an IBM or Apple Mac, which will have a word-processing programme built into it or available with it, but which will also be capable of accepting all kinds of other programmes, and of playing compact discs (including music). The most widely used word-processing programmes are Word and Wordperfect, and it is as well to choose the latest edition of one of them if you can. The package is quite likely to include a colour printer, a flatbed scanner, and a modem to connect you to the Internet and to allow you to send and receive e-mail. You will have a huge choice of fonts and sizes, the ability to draw pictures, a spellcheck, possibly a number of built-in games and other facilities, a wide range of colours in which you can print your work, and a hard disc which will store a huge amount of material (although you should always make copies of your work on floppies as a back-up or to send to other people).

It is almost certain, unless you are a computer buff and love playing with machines and exploring their possibilities, that you will use only a small part of the facilities available to you, especially when you first begin to use the computer. As time goes on, however, and you become familiar enough with it to experiment, you will probably find that it will be of use to you in more and more ways – the Internet can be invaluable for purposes of research, to give just one example.

If you want to be able to work when away from home, the answer will be to buy a portable computer (usually known as a 'laptop'), which you can use wherever you are, even on a train. This will store what you write, and you will be able to transfer it later to your main disc in the computer which you keep at home. If you have cash to spare, you can also buy a laptop printer, which would be ideal for working in a hotel room or anywhere away from your own home or place of work, but which would make the whole thing a bit bulky for use on public transport. Laptops are still quite expensive, and you could expect to pay upwards of £1000, and quite a lot extra for a laptop printer. No doubt prices will come down in due course.

Whether you use a simple word processor or a much more complicated set-up, you can always expand what it does by implanting additional facilities into the machine or by adding various bits on. For instance, if you buy a package which includes a colour printer, you may find that it is worth adding a second printer, which uses only black ink, because it will probably be both cheaper and quicker.

A word of warning: if you have not previously used a word processor or its big brother, the computer, once you have screwed up your courage and bought the thing, you will almost certainly regret it for the first two or three weeks. At first the word processor or computer and its workings will seem quite baffling. And, to make matters worse, most of the accompanying manuals appear to be written in gobbledegook and *never* have the answer to whatever problem you are wrestling with at the time. You will probably be in despair. Don't give up. Suddenly, it will all start to make sense, and before long the processes which you use regularly will become 'transparent' to you – which is to say that you will no longer even have to think about them, but will carry them out automatically. If, however, this does not happen, and you are still baffled, the solution is to find someone knowledgeable who will help.

Once you have become accustomed to your machine you are likely to become fond of it, and may also find that it becomes addictive. That is not a problem if you confine yourself to work, but computer programs come with games such as 'Minesweeper', 'Patience' (for which they use the American term 'Solitaire') and 'FreeCell'. If you are spending too much time playing about on your computer, give yourself a stern talking-to.

2 Books

Reference books may also be regarded as capital equipment. However, although most writers would consider a dictionary essential, there is no reason why you should spend a great deal of money on other reference books if you don't want to, or can't afford to. If possible, don't skimp on the dictionary, but get a good one, such as *The Shorter Oxford English Dictionary*, which gives derivations of words and an indication of when they first came into use. A thesaurus of synonyms and antonyms may be useful – the standard version is *Roget*, but you may find that others, especially those arranged more like dictionaries, are easier to use. You may want to consult a dictionary of quotations more often than you expect, and the same applies to an atlas. The splendid *Writers' and Artists' Yearbook* is an essential on the shelf, and it is not a bad idea to supplement it with its excellent, but less comprehensive, rival, *The Writer's Handbook*. If you are interested in any form of journalism or feature-writing, *Willings Press Guide* and *Benn's Media Guide* are other necessities. To have an encyclopædia may be something of a luxury and will demand a great deal of space, but nowadays encyclopædias are available on compact discs, which will be fine if you have the facility of loading a CD into your computer and consulting it on screen. Of course, you can always find virtually all the reference books that a writer might need by going to your Public Library, but I am sure that you don't need to be told how much more satisfactory it is to possess your own copies. Rather than buying large numbers of reference books yourself, think of those you most want when you are asked what you would like for Christmas!

3 Paper

Apart from paper, the only materials that a writer needs are pens and pencils for anything handwritten, ribbons and carbons if using an old-fashioned typewriter (do renew them regularly so that you produce sharp, legible results), and ink cartridges for a word processor or computer. All these are readily obtainable and comparatively inexpensive (although a colour cartridge for a colour printer can set you back quite a few pounds), and the kind of thing you buy will depend on the make of the equipment you use, and your own preference in the case of pens and pencils.

Paper, however, is different, because there is a wide choice. I am not referring here to stationery for your letters, to which I shall come shortly, but to the paper you use for your work. In general, if you are preparing work for eventual publication, you should stick to A4 sheets (297 x 210 mm) and should choose a white paper. Coloured papers, like coloured typewriter ribbons, are for private use only. Paper is available in various weights, expressed in 'gsm' (grams per square metre); 80 gsm is acceptable, but 70 gsm is the most suitable weight, while 90 gsm is thicker than necessary (although I find myself using it simply because it is considerably cheaper in my local stationer's). So-called 'bank' paper, which is usually quite flimsy, is ideal if you want to make carbon copies or draft print-outs of your work. Since anything which you send out for an editor's consideration should be typed or printed on one side of the paper only (and in double spacing, of course), it seems a good idea to get into the habit and produce drafts in the same style, but many authors use the other side of their drafts for further drafts or for scrap paper.

If you are submitting work to the United States, editors there like authors to use the American standard size of 280 x 217 mm, but paper of this size is not easy to come by in Britain, except in the form of continuous paper for use on certain printers attached to word processors or computers (the famous old Amstrad used continuous paper of this kind, although it was also possible to feed in separate sheets). Although the Americans prefer their size of paper, they are accustomed to Brits using our own size, so it is not a major issue.

4 Insurance

You may wish to consider seriously the insurance of your equipment and its attachments. It is standard practice for such equipment to be insured against malfunction by the vendor or the manufacturers for 12 months after purchase, and you will almost certainly be offered various insurance schemes when that period is about to expire. Repairs can be extremely costly, and often a complete replacement is necessary; moreover, if something does go wrong, you will want it put right as soon as possible – authors who are used to working on a computer usually go right round the bend if it becomes unusable – and insurance usually guarantees a quick response. On the other hand, although we live in a throw-away society, most of the equipment now on the market can be relied on to function effectively for a considerable time. Whether you take up the offers therefore depends on your personal finances and on your attitude to such matters. The cautious take out insurance; the gamblers take the risk.

The insurances that we have been considering are usually concerned only with the machine, or a part of it, ceasing to function properly. Since a computer can be a valuable piece of equipment, it is worth considering taking out an insurance which will also cover theft, maybe identifying it as a special item on your house contents policy. Even if you are fully covered, it is not the possibility of having the computer stolen when you are away from home which is the greatest worry, at least as far as I am concerned. I could bear the loss of the computer itself with comparative equanimity, because it is replaceable, but I cannot contemplate with anything but panic the possible loss of any work in progress stored on the machine's hard disc. So when I go away I take with me floppy discs holding copies of those things which I would hate to lose.

5 Stationery
You will undoubtedly need writing paper and envelopes, folders and probably a stapler and Sellotape and similar bits and pieces, and various pens and pencils, even if you work on a typewriter or word processor. If you have a word processor, you will not need to have your stationery printed with your name and address – you can set up a heading which will appear automatically on your letters. A business card can be impressive, especially if it is engraved rather than printed, but it is hardly necessary, and those little sticky labels will be adequate.

Miscellaneous costs

There are many incidental costs for which you should budget if you are going to take your writing seriously.

Unless you live or work in London and near to the areas where publishers have their offices, you will probably incur considerable expense on postage. Typescripts of books are heavy things, and it costs a lot to mail them, especially if you enclose return postage, without which your typescript, if rejected, will probably be binned rather than returned to you. Fortunately, most publishers nowadays are willing, indeed happier, to consider synopses and specimen chapters rather than the whole thing. Even so, it is very easy to spend a lot of money on postage, even if you are not writing books but are concentrating on articles which occupy perhaps no more than a couple of pages. It is not only a question of postage of the material you have written, but of follow-up letters and general correspondence.

You will probably also have to make various telephone, fax and e-mail calls in relation to your work, although this may not be as expensive as the mailing costs. A telephone nowadays seems to be a necessity, unless you are very hard-up, and, as far as a writer is concerned, will certainly be useful if you need to communicate with agents and editors, and perhaps for some of your research, in addition to its ordinary day-to-day uses. Whether you also need a mobile phone is entirely up to you. A fax machine has a great many advantages, particularly in the speed with which it works and its photocopying function. E-mail (electronic mail), use of the Internet, and perhaps your own website, are currently moving rapidly from the status of luxuries into that of necessities, as more and more people have and use the facilities available.

Writing is notoriously a lonely business, and one of the principal reasons for joining associations for writers is that it gives you the opportunity of meeting people with the same interests as yours. But joining means paying a subscription, even if it is no more than the comparatively modest charge made by the local Writers' Circle.

You will need to keep abreast of current trends in your particular field, and one of the ways of doing so is by subscribing to the various magazines or journals which bring you such up-to-date information.

Research

Some tutors of Creative Writing have a habit of telling you to 'write about what you know'. That may be good advice for complete beginners, and it certainly applies to most non-fiction, but it tends to undervalue the writer's imagination, and to ignore the possibility of learning what you don't already know by means of research. To give just two examples, H. R. F. Keating had not been to India until after several of his crime stories set in that country had been published, and John Trenhaile had written in an apparently extremely knowledgeable way about Moscow without having set foot in that city.

Very few authors can manage altogether without doing any research; for some it is a major part of writing. Research can involve travel, the purchase of books, entertainment, telephone calls and postage, and the expense can amount to a considerable sum. Even the cheapest form of research – a visit to your local Public Library – may cost you a bus fare or petrol for your car.

In almost every case, research expenses are the author's responsibility. They are tax deductible against your income from writing if the Inland Revenue accepts you as a working author (see Chapter 7), although you would probably not get away with it if you tried to claim all your holiday expenses as research. That tax concession is about as far as it goes in respect of any clawback of your research expenses. If you have dreams of a benevolent publisher giving you vast sums to compensate for what you spend on research, forget it – especially if your book is a novel.

Publishers are sometimes willing to help with the expenses of research for a non-fiction book, but only if the cost of the research is more than the author can be expected to bear, if the publisher is as eager to publish the book as the author is to write it, and, above all, if the publisher can see a really handsome sale for it. An obvious case is an exceptional travel book of some kind, and the project will undoubtedly have been discussed and commissioned before the writer actually incurs the expenses. If the book is already complete when the publisher buys it, what has already been spent on research is the author's look-out.

If the publisher does agree to subsidise your research, beware of any suggestion that the payment should be in the form of an increase in the advance against your royalties. That would mean, in effect, that you were simply getting a loan, which would in due course be paid off by your earnings. To be of real benefit any contribution from the publisher should be an entirely separate, non-returnable sum, and should be indicated formally as such in the agreement.

Permissions

If you quote any copyright material in your book, you must get permission to do so. Since copyright in the European Community and the United States lasts for seventy years after the author's death, you may quote as freely as you like from most of the Victorian writers and those who lived in earlier centuries, but make sure that the date of death was more than seventy years ago, and that the work was not first published posthumously (in which case the copyright lasts for 70 years from first publication) or has not been revised in some way which would extend the copyright (any such extension will be indicated on the reverse of the title page).

Permission to quote is normally obtainable from the publisher of the quoted work, or in some cases from the author or his or her agent. An approach to the publisher in the first place will usually be successful, but in any case should tell you where to apply if the work is not controlled by the publisher. When you quote copyright material, it is necessary to include in the published version of your work an acknowledgement of the source of the quoted matter (usually citing the title of the work, the author, the publisher and often the year of publication). Whoever has the right to give permission to quote will tell you in what form the acknowledgement should appear, and what fee will be payable. Sometimes the person granting permission demands a complimentary copy of the published book.

It is not normally necessary to apply for permissions until you have a commitment to publish from a publisher, nor is it advisable, because the publisher will be able to tell you what permissions to apply for – for instance, if the book is to be published only in the British market, it may not be worth seeking world rights in respect of the quoted material. However, it is certainly sensible to make an enquiry at an early stage about the possible cost if you want to quote extensively, because the fees may be so expensive that you will decide to omit some of the material which you proposed to include. It is worth noting that the fees charged for poetry and especially for lyrics of popular songs are often astonishingly high. Remember, too, that artwork and photographs are also subject to copyright, and illustrative works by famous artists may be very expensive. If you want to reproduce paintings by artists who have been dead for seventy years or more, they may be out of copyright, but you will find that the national galleries which own them will charge very highly for their use; such fees are not in fact charged in respect of copyright, but for access to the originals.

Do not be misled in respect of textual quotations by what is often known as 'fair dealing'. This is a convention under which you are allowed to quote without seeking permission or paying a fee a single prose extract of not more than 400 words or a series of extracts, none of which should exceed 300 words, totalling no more than 800 words, or up to 40 lines from a poem, provided that the passage quoted does not form more than a quarter of the poem. Of course, you must still give a full acknowledgement of the source of the material. The problem is that legally you may use such extracts without obtaining permission only in the course of a review or for purposes of criticism. In practice, most publishers and authors are unlikely to cause any difficulties in respect of a really brief quotation even if it cannot be said to be used for critical purposes, but if the passage concerned is of any length (i.e. more than a short phrase) it is advisable to clear it with the copyright holders.

Fair dealing does not apply to anthologies, for which permission must be sought in respect of all copyright material used.

The clearance of permissions is normally the author's responsibility, although in certain rare circumstances (because, for instance, the author is not resident in the country) the publisher will agree to undertake clearance on his or her behalf. The cost of permissions, which can sometimes be considerable, as already mentioned, is invariably the author's responsibility. In an exceptional case when the publisher may agree to pay all or part of the fees, you will need, as suggested earlier in respect of research, to beware of the suggestion that the advance against royalties should be increased in order to subsidise the permission fees.

Illustrations

Most of what has been said about permissions applies to illustrations. You will need to seek permission for the inclusion of any illustrations unless you originate them yourself. Before doing so you should check with the publisher whether there is any restriction on the number to be included, whether any of them can be in full colour, and so on. An enormous range of photographs is available from photo agencies, to which you can go yourself, although some publishers employ a picture-researcher to do this job, but you will almost certainly still be responsible for the fees. Publishers will sometimes agree to pay fees for the use of illustrations up to a specified amount, after which the costs become the author's responsibility.

It is worth remembering, by the way, that the copyright of photographs lies with the photographer (or the employer in the case, for instance, of a staff photographer working for a newspaper), not with the subject. Even if you ask a local photographer to take a portrait of yourself for publicity purposes, you do not count as the employer, and the copyright is still with the person who was behind the camera.

In the case of maps or diagrams, if you cannot produce them yourself to an acceptable standard, the publisher will commission an artist to prepare them, and may well ask you to bear the cost, or at least to share in it. If the book is to be heavily illustrated, as with a step-by-step manual of some kind, or a children's book, the publisher will probably commission the photographer or artist; you will not have to share the costs in such cases, but the size of your royalty is likely to be affected by the extra expenses incurred by the publisher.

Index

If you have written a book, and it requires an index (as most works of non-fiction do), you usually have the option of preparing the index yourself, or of having the job done by a professional. Your publisher may have strong views on the matter, especially if the book is long and complex, when the work of a competent indexer would be preferable to that of the inexpert author. The contract may specify which method is to be used, and, in a few cases will also state whether the publisher will bear any of the cost if an outside indexer is employed.

It may be very tempting to prepare your own index – after all it looks a simple enough job, and having written the book you know more about it than anyone else. But it is not as easy as you may imagine. If you have not indexed a book previously, at least you should bear in mind three fairly simple rules: the first is always to put yourself in the reader's place and think of what headings that person might be looking for, so you use clear, immediately identifiable entries, and do not include entries which are unlikely to mean anything until after you have looked them up, and possibly not even then; secondly, try not to put too many page references against a single entry in the index, but sub-divide such entries into specific aspects of the main subject; and thirdly, do not include entries for names or events which are mentioned only in passing in the text and have no major significance.

The best course of action, however, will be to go to the Society of Indexers. Membership of the Society is confined to those who have demonstrated their competence in such work. Many of them have specialist knowledge in certain fields, so that you might, for instance, ask for someone with more than a passing knowledge of French Literature if that happens to be the subject of your book. It must be pointed out, however, that because the work is not only difficult and exacting, but cannot be rushed, the charges made by members of the Society of Indexers are not cheap – in fact, the NUJ recommends a fee for simple indexing of £13.80 an hour, which can mount into a sizeable sum indeed. Generally speaking, you will be presented with an excellent Index, but since it will be appearing in *your* book, you have responsibility for it, and it is as well to check carefully that it is satisfactory in every respect.

If you are unwilling, or for some reason unable, to take any responsibility for the index, the publishers will usually be prepared to do so, will commission a professional to undertake the job, and will expect to charge you for it, and this can make a very large hole in your earnings from the book. It is always worth asking the publishers whether there is a chance of sharing the costs, and, depending on the importance of the book, you may be fortunate. In rare cases the publishers may even agree to stand the whole cost.

3. Submissions

Market research

If you want to sell the material which you have written, you must know the market.

Research is essential to keep abreast of what is going on in whatever medium interests you. That implies a great deal of reading, even if you are working in a field such as television or the theatre which is primarily visual – you will learn as much or more from reading successful material in the genre as from watching it.

Market research will also help you to discover what length of material is likely to be accepted, whether there are any taboos (for instance, about the use of the so-called 'four-letter words'), whether the language you use, and the structure of sentences and paragraphs, should be extremely simple or more complex. These questions apply whatever the genre of your work. However, some forms of writing make their own particular demands. For instance, if you are writing plays you need to be aware of the importance of keeping the settings simple (especially if you are writing for the theatre, where a single permanent set is nowadays highly desirable), and of avoiding a large cast (the more characters you include, the more expensive the production becomes, because actors have to be paid). Television has a wider scope for settings, but even then you should remember that outdoor scenes are usually much more expensive, and difficult, to film. You are much more free with radio, which can take you in the listener's imagination to anywhere in the world, without increasing the costs, but even in that medium you will probably do better with a fairly small number of actors (the longer the cast list, the more difficult it will be for the listener to remember who they all are).

It is vital to make sure that you send your work to the kind of potential purchaser who might be interested in it. Market research in this area is quite easily done – you need to look at what is published or performed and by whom and, in the case of books, to ask for relevant information from booksellers and librarians, and, for all genres, to pick the brains of anyone who may have experience in the field. Use the *Writers' and Artists' Yearbook* to supplement the information you acquire – especially to check whether the potential purchasers in whom you are interested are prepared to consider material sent to them direct by the author, rather than through an agent. If you are aiming at newspapers, consult *Willings Press Guide*. Make yourself a list of the concerns to which you will send your work.

In the present age of conglomerates, many well-known publishing firms are merely divisions (known in the trade as 'imprints') of the parent company. For instance, Anchor, Bantam, Bantam Press, Bantam Children's Books, Black Swan, Corgi, Doubleday, Doubleday Children's Books and Partridge Press are all imprints of Transworld Publishers, which itself is a division of Random House Group, and that in turn is a subsidiary of the German concern, Bertelsmann AG. The various imprints of the conglomerates, and those which sometimes exist in much smaller, independent publishing houses, usually cater for different markets. It is a useful part of your market research to check which imprint would be most interested in your work. In some cases it may be worth your while to submit your work to more than one imprint of a conglomerate, because their editorial departments act independently, but in other groups, a single submission will be considered by all the imprints. The *Writers' and Artists' Yearbook* contains full information about which houses are imprints of which larger companies, and you can find out which are editorially independent by putting an enquiry to the parent company.

While you are studying your market, look out for a gap in it which you think you might be able to fill. Many hugely successful writers, from Chaucer to Shakespeare, from Samuel Richardson to Mickey Spillane have done exactly that. Nearly all Claire Rayner's non-fiction books and television programmes have resulted from her ability to pinpoint a gap in the market, and Bill Bryson realised, because no-one else had done it, that there was room for a book in which an American took an affectionate look at the oddities of British social customs. Is there a magazine which might be interested in a regular column on a subject which it does not presently cover, but which it should?

As a teacher, are you aware of the need for a textbook which is different from those currently available? Could you fill a regular slot in a chat programme on local radio to which listeners could phone with questions on your particular subject? Finding a gap can be very rewarding. Equally, although it is sometimes possible to jump on to the bandwaggon of whatever is currently flavour of the month (if you will forgive so mixed a metaphor), it is often best to avoid an overcrowded market. If you can forecast future trends, you are almost certainly on a winner, but it is very difficult to make predictions unless you happen to be Mystic Meg and in possession of a really reliable crystal ball.

One final but important point on the subject of identifying your market: while it is only sensible to write with the market in mind, you should never allow yourself to be untrue to your own feelings and convictions. To write, for instance, a steamy sex scene in a novel, simply because you think that will make it more saleable, although you yourself find it distasteful, is likely to lead only to a piece of contrived, unnatural writing, which any experienced editor will immediately recognise as unpublishable.

It will undoubtedly help you to read not only the work of successful contemporary writers, but also the magazines devoted to various trades, such as *The Bookseller*, which covers the publishing scene as well as bookselling, or *The Stage* for anything to do with drama. If your interest lies mainly in writing articles or short stories for magazines, *Writers News*, *Writers' Forum* and other similar publications contain up-to-date information about new magazines and those which are folding. *The Author*, *The Writers' Newsletter* and *The Journalist*, the regular publications for members of the Society of Authors, the Writers' Guild of Great Britain and The National Union of Journalists respectively, can be very helpful, and the same can be said of the journals put out by other associations for writers in specialist genres. In any magazine that you read, don't forget to look at the advertisements, which will help you to identify the market. And an immense amount of information of use to all manner of writers is to be found in the *Writers' and Artists' Yearbook*.

Typescript

Your material must, of course, be typed, on one side of the paper only, and with margins of at least 2.5 cm (1 in.) all round the text. Double spacing is used for books, short stories and magazine or newspaper features, poetry is laid out exactly as the poem should appear if printed, and work in dramatic form uses single spacing for the dialogue, separating one character's speech from the next with a blank line, while the name of the character speaking is shown in capital letters on the left-hand side of the page and stage directions are in italics. The BBC's book, *Writing for the BBC*, gives clear instructions on the layout of television and radio scripts.

We have not yet arrived at a point when it is expected that submissions will be made initially in the form of a disc produced on your computer, but that time will come. In the meantime, if you send a disc, it should be accompanied by hard copy (i.e. a print-out), and probably sent in Text Only or Rich Text Format.

Enquiry letters

If, before submitting material for consideration, you write a letter of enquiry, always enclose a stamped addressed envelope for the reply, and if you require the return of submitted material, always enclose the necessary postage. Keep the enquiry letter short and businesslike, but not so short that it gives virtually no information about the material that you are trying to sell. And do not fail to give details of anything which may make your work more interesting to the person who will read it – for instance, its topicality, or your own expertise. In the case of a book, perhaps you can promise a guaranteed sale to members of a specialist society, or an introduction by a famous person, or (probably the best recommendation of all) that your book is different from any available competitive work, because it uses an entirely new approach, or is aimed at a different market, or has more illustrations, or for some other good reason – but do make sure that your claim is valid.

All the above applies equally if you are trying to find an agent, rather than going directly to a potential buyer. Agents do not usually handle features or short stories or poetry or anything less than what might be called 'full-length' material. If instead your writing is of the kind which would interest an agent, it is certainly worth trying to get one. The snag is that it is extremely difficult to find an agent who is prepared to take on an unknown writer, and you may do better on your own. If you get an acceptance, it will be much easier to find an agent at that stage and it will still be worth using one (see pages 101–6).

Features for newspapers and magazines

Although there is no reason why you shouldn't write a feature (you may think of it as an 'article', but that is a layman's term) and submit it to a suitable newspaper or magazine without making any preliminary approach, it is advisable to write first to the editor asking if he or she would be interested in a piece on such-and-such a subject. In your (brief and businesslike) letter you will naturally explain why you think the editor might be interested and what your qualifications for writing the piece are. If you are approaching a newspaper or magazine for the first time, it will be as well to mention, if you can, any previous instances when your work has been published (although the editor will probably not be much impressed if you can claim no more than publication in the local church magazine). Incidentally, you do not need to be a member of a journalists' union – newspapers and magazines regularly accept work from freelancers.

You will nearly always increase your chances of acceptance if you tell the editor that you can provide good illustrations, but they must be really good, and capable of clear reproduction, and they must be relevant and add an extra element of interest to your piece.

There are three replies that the editor can make: a commission, a rejection, or a willingness to look at the feature when completed.

In the first case – a commission – the reply will state the wordage required and the fee (or at least it should); you then go ahead and write the piece, if it is not already completed. Do so promptly, and send it in with an invoice and a note quoting the date and content of the editor's reply to your enquiry letter, and, unless the editor has changed his or her mind or your work is not of a good enough standard, the feature should appear in due course. If the editor does not accept it, you may be asked to re-work it, or you may be offered a 'kill fee' (see page 60). Be prepared in any case for the fact that your work may be edited (which is done more often for reasons of space available than for the sake of messing about with your deathless prose).

A feature which has been accepted for publication should not be kept indefinitely by a magazines or newspaper without publication, so if the months go by without the material appearing, you should ask for payment forthwith.

If the editor rejects your idea, look for somewhere else to send it and start again.

And if, without making any commitment, the editor asks to see the feature when completed, again, when you send it in, include in the covering letter a reminder of that fact that 'this is the piece which you asked to see'.

Short stories

The market for short stories is more or less limited nowadays to magazines and to collections in book form by different authors, but usually on a single theme. The collections of one author's short stories which do appear in book form are nearly all by established writers who regularly achieve high sales with their full-length work.

While it seems to be best to write an enquiry letter first in the case of features, this is not really necessary for short stories submitted to magazines. Make sure that your story is suitable for the magazine at which you are aiming, both in subject matter and length, find out the name of the fiction editor, and send the story off. But naturally it is worth mentioning in your covering note any previous successes which you have had.

One other market for short stories, which may be worth trying, is radio. The BBC has given up its Morning Story (and the afternoon version) but it still occasionally finds room for a story, and it is also possible that a local radio station might be interested.

As with features, if your short story is accepted for publication, do not allow the work to be kept indefinitely without either a firm commitment to publish or payment in advance, but you will have to take into consideration the topicality of your piece – if you have written a Christmas story, for instance, you may have to wait for twelve months if it has missed this year's Christmas issue. In such a case it would be advisable to send the editor a reminder, round about August or September, that the time for its publication is approaching.

Fillers for magazines and newspapers

Fillers (short paragraphs, often humorous, which an editor can use to fill a empty space on a page) are best submitted in bulk, as it were. There is no real need to write an enquiry letter first, but do make sure that the newspaper or magazine which you are targeting does in fact use fillers (there is a very long list of such publications in the *Writers' and Artists' Yearbook*). Send in half a dozen at a time, watch out to see if they are used and then ask for payment if it does not arrive.

Books

It used to be de rigueur to send a brief letter of enquiry first, enclosing a stamped addressed envelope, of course, to ask whether someone in your chosen publishing house would be prepared to consider your material, but it seems nowadays that you might just as well submit the work without a preliminary enquiry, unless the firm's entry in the *Writers' and Artists' Yearbook* specifically asks for a letter first. It is very easy for an editor to say 'no' to a letter or a telephone call, but if you send the material, or a part of it, at least there is then a chance that what you have written will be looked at. It is always worth making a telephone call to find out to which department, and preferably to which person, you should address your sub-mission, but don't expect to do more than that – no-one in the publisher's office will want to talk to you at that stage, so just get your vital bit of information and then politely ring off.

For many years now it has been possible to sell a non-fiction book to a publisher on the basis of a synopsis and specimen chapters, so that it is not necessary to write the whole book before trying to find a publisher for it and, with luck, being commissioned to complete it. Indeed, the publisher may welcome the fact that the whole book has not yet been written, since it gives the editor the opportunity to make suggestions about what should or should not be included.

In the letter accompanying the submission or as part of the typescript, give details concerning the illustrations, diagrams, maps, index or anything of that sort which the book will need, and say whether you can provide whatever is required. Don't indi-cate that you have illustrative material available unless it is of a really high standard, which will reproduce well. Be prepared to listen to the publisher's advice about the number and style of illus-trations and other extras which should be included in the book.

The synopsis-and-specimen-chapters approach used not to be acceptable for fiction, but nowadays most publishers prefer it. How many chapters should you send? Two or three, according to length. In my time as an editor I always preferred to have the first three chapters: Chapter 1 must be there, because it is essential to show that the opening of your novel is strong and that it will immediately grab the reader's interest; Chapters 2 and 3 show how well you are developing the characters and the plot. If I were sent, let us say, Chapters 3, 8 and 17, I always suspected that the author had chosen them because he or she considered them to be better than the others, which suggested an uneven texture to the story as a whole. Even worse is the practice which some authors indulge in of sending a few single pages taken from various parts of the book – it is invariably true that they are the only bits of the book worth any attention at all, and they are usually so awful that it is easily possible to guess how dire the rest of the book must be.

As for the synopsis, the question which most would-be authors ask is how long it should be. Obviously, it will depend to some extent on the length of the novel, and the complexity of the plot and sub-plots. In general, it is as well to restrict it, if you can, to three or four double-spaced A4 pages – anything longer becomes too much of a chore for the editor, while anything much shorter is inclined to be far too skimpy. If you are a writer who plans in advance, your own synopsis will probably be far too detailed to be used, other than as a basis which you will edit down to a length which will not put too much strain on a poor, overworked editor's willingness to be interested.

Make sure too that you send a synopsis and not a blurb. A blurb is a sales pitch, meant to titillate the reader's interest without revealing all that happens in the book. In contrast, the editor wants the synopsis to contain the whole story, so that it can be seen whether the author has handled the plot effectively, whether the solutions to the problems raised in the course of the narrative are credible, and so on.

If you want to write a children's book, the question of illustrations will probably arise. Don't attempt to illustrate the book yourself unless you are a really competent artist, and if you want to suggest a friend or relation as the illustrator, do apply the same criteria to them and their work.

Poetry

If you have on hand enough poems to make a book, then follow the advice above under the heading Books. But if you are aiming at the little magazines which publish poetry, you will be able to find a number of possible outlets. Many of them special-ise in some way, and because they are publishing contemporary work, lean towards the experimental in language and form. Having checked that the magazine publishes the kind of poetry that you write, send off a batch of poems – preferably four to six, which will be sufficient to show your style and capabilities. It is not necessary to write an enquiry letter first, but do enclose a covering letter and s.a.e. if you want the material back. Put your name and address on every sheet, so that each poem is clearly labelled as yours.

The Writer's Handbook publishes a list of poetry magazines and presses. There are other markets which are worth trying: radio (especially local radio), newspapers (including the nationals), and the Internet. Listen to the broadcasts or read the papers and see if your material might fit in, and if so just send it off, remembering again to enclose a covering letter and, if you want the poems back, s.a.e.

As for the Internet, you could either make your own Home Page and publish your poetry there, or you could submit it to one of the increasing number of Internet poetry magazines; find them by using one of the search engines and then submit your material by e-mail.

Plays for the theatre

As with most forms of writing, the standard advice as far as plays written for the theatre are concerned is to find yourself an agent, and you will need one who specialises in plays. This is often easier said than done, and it may pay you to try direct sub-missions, and wait to get an agent until you already have the offer of a production, which at that stage will be essential anyway.

There are many possibilities. Your aim of getting the play put on in the West End of London straightaway is probably some-thing of a pipe dream, especially if you do not have an agent – several managements will consider submissions only if they come from an agent. Still in London, there are companies which specialise in the production of new plays (usually of a some-what experimental nature) such as the Royal Court and Hampstead Theatres. Outside London there are repertory theatres and small touring companies, and some of the latter specialise in plays which appeal to a particular audience (for example, plays with a political theme, or which deal with a social problem of some kind). A further alternative is to send your play to a star actor (but you will need to be sure that the part is likely to have a considerable attraction for him or her), or to a director who is looking for a new play (if you know of such a person). Drama schools and amateur companies will sometimes be delighted to be given the chance of producing a new play, and not the least benefit of this approach is that when you see the play performed in front of a live audience, you may realise that alterations are needed to improve its impact.

As with most submissions in any genre, find out, if you can, to whom your work should be sent, and whether it should be in the form of a completed script or an outline with or without specimen material. The *Writers' and Artists' Yearbook* contains a list of theatrical producers, with some details about them and their requirements.

Do not expect a quick reply when you submit a play for consideration. Theatre managements are mostly even slower than book publishers and a wait of three to six months is not unusual.

Play publishers

If your play is presented at a commercial theatre in London, your agent will probably make arrangements with a publisher to produce it in book form. But if you have not had that success and do not have an agent, there is no reason why you should not submit the work to a play publisher. The current *Writers' and Artists' Yearbook* lists more than twenty publishers of plays. Some of these are general publishers who bring out an occasional drama (usually of a literary nature) in book form, but others, like Samuel French or Warner/Chappell Plays, specialise in plays. Such publishers will also be the main market for one-act plays, which are rarely performed in the professional theatre, but are still popular with amateur companies. As with books, the submission process can start with a letter of enquiry or you can simply send your play off without any preliminary skirmishing, provided that you do your market research properly.

Television

It is very difficult for a writer who is a newcomer to break into the television world. The advice, as always, is that it is best to get an agent, and the snag, as always, is that it isn't easy for an unknown to find one. However, if you manage, by a direct submission, to interest a television or film company in your work, you should have little difficulty at that stage in getting on to an agent's list.

Make sure that your scenario is possible in terms of cost, and that it is presented in the approved style (Gerald Kelsey's book *Writing for Television* is very helpful). Remember, too, that the slots for plays on television are usually 30, 60, 90 or 120 minutes in length, and make sure that you are neither under-running nor over-running. If you are writing for the ITV channels, you will have to leave time for the advertisements, and make sure that your drama has natural breaks in which those ads can be screened.

The possible outlets for teleplays in Britain, as you will be aware, are the BBC, ITV and the Satellite channels, and you can select whichever seems, because of the content of your work, to be most appropriate. It is acceptable to send the material off without a preliminary enquiry, but with a covering letter and stamps for the return of the material. However, if you write an initial letter of enquiry and receive a reply asking to see the script, that will mean that the teleplay will not be put at the bottom of the slushpile, like all those which are sent unsolicited, and will be considered more promptly.

Alternatively, you can approach one of the producing organisations listed in the *Writers' and Artists' Yearbook*. In this case, it is advisable to start by sending an enquiry letter with a synopsis of your project, but do read the entries in the *Yearbook* with care, because many of the production companies will accept submissions only via an agent. The synopsis should be quite brief, but if you are proposing a series – perhaps a sitcom – you will need to give information about the various ideas you have to carry your characters beyond the pilot episode. Incidentally, as already mentioned earlier, if you are aiming at the BBC, you will find their own handbook, *Writing for the BBC*, very helpful.

Another possibility is writing an episode for a series, such as *Casualty* or *The Bill*, in which the characters, whom you might think of as the staff, remain the same (although their relation-ships may develop), but the plot of the episode is a new one, involving characters who will probably appear in this one teleplay only. The problem is that many of the producers of such programmes will not look at samples of scripts using the on-going characters, since they do not wish to be accused of lifting ideas from submissions made on spec. The best advice is to write first to the Plays Department and ask whether they would be prepared to consider a submission, and in which form and under which restrictions. The same would apply if you want to become one of the team of writers who create the scripts for serials, such as *Coronation Street* or *EastEnders*.

What about adapting an existing novel, whether classic or contemporary, for the small screen? The television companies almost always use experienced writers, but even such gods were once beginners, so if you have a good idea for such an adaptation, send it in. It will probably be best to stick to the classic novels (if there are any left which have not yet been televised), because you will not have the copyright problems which would arise with contemporary fiction.

Films

Films are an even more difficult proposition than television, which is subsidised by the television licence fee or by the advertisements, whereas films require private investment on a very substantial scale. An agent really is a necessity, not only at the preliminary stage, but to oversee the grant of an option, and the complete contract, and to ensure that your rights are respected at all times. However, there is still the possibility of a direct submission to production companies, as outlined above for teleplays.

One possibility is that a producer will like the idea contained in your proposal, but not want you to be involved in writing the screenplay – film companies often employ their own screenwriters to adapt material from an outside source. You would then be paid for the idea only. It is unlikely that they will pinch your idea, although, since ideas are not copyright, it could happen. Some writers, who are very suspicious in this respect, go to considerable lengths to safeguard their work so that they can, if necessary, cry 'Plagiarism!' and demand redress. Probably the best defence against anyone plundering your idea is to dream up something which is so original that it would be really difficult for anyone else to pretend to have been inspired with the same concept.

Follow the procedures above if you are thinking of an adaptation for the screen of an already published work. If it is a matter of adapting your own book, your agent or your publisher will handle any negotiations, and it may be possible for you to write the teleplay, provided that you can convince the producer of your competence in that direction.

Radio

The BBC still dominates the scene, both nationwide and through local radio, but there are now a great many independent stations. Although much of air-time is taken up by music, the spoken word is still regularly in demand and, apart from the chatter of DJs and the live interviews and phone-ins, most of it is scripted. Indeed, there is great scope for the writer, whether the material is journalistic, or a talk, or a play. Programmes are always produced by someone and/or directed by someone, and the information can readily be found simply by listening to the programmes. If you fail to find the names of producers or directors, you can make an approach to the stations. The *Writers' and Artists' Yearbook* lists both the BBC local stations and the dozens of independents, and helpfully singles out among the latter those which are open to the submission of material, although most of them still like to have a letter of enquiry first.

When you have done your market research, send your material to a producer or editor who you think might be interested. If the material has a particular local or regional flavour, it will obviously be sensible to try the regional outlets rather than the national broadcasters. One useful tip is that if you submit material to any of the BBC's national programmes and your work is rejected, you can still try it out on regional or local BBC stations, but if it has been turned down regionally or locally, then it is no use sending it to the parent body.

Any material written for radio needs to be of a suitable length for the slot at which you are aiming. If you are writing a play, for instance, you will need to ensure that it runs for the right length of time for the slots which are used – perhaps 28 or 29 minutes, or 58 or 59 minutes (the odd minutes leaving room for announcements before and after the broadcast).

Be prepared for a very long wait before you get a verdict. Even the regional and local stations are often snowed under with unsolicited submissions, and it does appear that any material which comes in is carefully looked at before a decision is made (which is reassuring, and more than can be said for some of the other media).

Simultaneous submissions

In the past – say thirty years ago – any writer suspected of having sent work for consideration to more than one potential buyer at the same time would have had the typescript returned smartly. It made life difficult for an author, because publishers often took a really unconscionable time before coming to a decision (and many still do); if the work were the kind of borderline case on which a publisher would want several readings and the preparation of a number of costings, even the more efficient houses might retain the typescript for weeks, or even months, on end before reaching a final verdict. In either case, if the submission were finally rejected, the author would then have to start the submission process all over again. There was the additional problem that if, perhaps in the light of comments on the work, the writer felt it necessary to produce a revised typescript, it would probably mean having the whole thing retyped and, in any case, there was a limit to the number of legible carbon copies which could be produced at one go.

The delays in reaching a verdict still exist, but happily most publishers no longer refuse to countenance simultaneous submissions, and this has come about for two reasons. Firstly, it seems that most buyers in the various markets have become aware, as a result of pressure from the organisations which represent authors, that such delays are unfair, and secondly, the availability of the personal computer means that revisions can easily be made and as many readable copies of the work produced as needed, at little cost, and with virtually no effort once the work is complete on disc.

In the 1980s the Publishers Association produced a Code of Practice. Regarding submissions, it promised that unsolicited submissions would be dealt with promptly (within six weeks), and it recognised simultaneous submission as a fact of life, although it indicated that it would be acceptable only if the publishers were told that other houses would be considering the work at the same time. Recently, however, the Society of Authors has suggested that you should not bother to give such information. Why not? Firstly, because many publishers still take months to deal with the slushpile (books submitted directly by the author, rather than through an agent), and secondly, because it seems likely that it may prejudice the book's chances if a publisher is told that other houses are looking at the material at the same time.

33

What if the result of simultaneous submission is simultaneous offers from different publishers? You think yourself lucky and make a choice. One of the potential purchasers will be pleased and the others will not, so choose carefully.

Waiting for a verdict

Whether the verdict for which you are waiting is in respect of an enquiry letter or on the submission itself, you should be aware that very few organisations to which written material is submitted are likely to respond rapidly (although, of course, if you are an established writer you will certainly not wait nearly so long as a beginner). You might think that a simple reply to a simple letter of enquiry could come back to you by return of post, but I don't think you should be surprised if a couple of weeks go by without a response – at least, there is the possibility that your letter has been more carefully considered than an immediate return might suggest. And, regrettably, there are some discourteous people who will not reply at all, even though you have included a stamped, addressed envelope.

When it comes to submission of your work itself, you may have to wait for as long as six weeks or more. There are two main reasons for the delay: first of all, you must remember that every day of the year hundreds of would-be authors are busily parcelling up their typescripts and sending them off for consideration. When they are received in an office, they go into a queue, which can only be looked at after priority has been given to authors already on the list and to agented work; secondly, the material may require more than one reading. Patience is essential. If you hear nothing after six weeks, you could send a polite letter asking for information about the material, and if six months go by without response, demand its return.

4. Copyright and Contracts

Copyright

Anything that you write which is original to you (that is to say, it has not been copied from someone else's writings) is copyright, and remains copyright within the European Union and in the USA for the remainder of your life and for 70 years after your death, or 70 years from the time of publication if it is first published or broadcast or performed posthumously. The 70-year period begins at the end of the year in which you die or in which the posthumous publication takes place. In most developed countries outside the EU, you are similarly protected under the Berne Convention during your lifetime and for at least 50 years after your death (the period is longer in some countries).

Copyright applies not only to written work, but to the spoken word when recorded in any form and by any means. It does not have to have been published, so long as it is set down in manuscript (handwriting), typescript, on tape or disc or on the Internet.

The fact that your work is copyright means that no one may reproduce it without your permission. Equally, of course, every other author's work is copyright unless he or she died more than 70 years ago, and you may not quote such 'in copyright' work without permission, except in certain very limited circumstances (see pages 16–18).

Your copyrights are valuable and you should never sell them or assign them to someone else, unless you wish perhaps to make a present of the copyright in one or more of your works to someone in your family. After your death, your copyrights form part of your estate and will pass into the ownership of your heirs, according to your Will. If you do sell the copyright in any of your works to a commercial concern, the purchaser may go on publishing it and licensing others to bring it out in various forms, and in general exploiting it, without paying you a single penny as a further fee or in royalties or as a share of subsidiary rights. If the purchaser is honest, you may not lose all the rewards you should have, but even a scrupulous publisher or management is not bound to make any additional payment, and if you are unlucky enough to have sold to someone with no conscience, you will get nothing. What is more, you would have no redress by going to law. Even if the sum for which you sold the copyright is a substantial one, you are quite likely to lose out, and may do so very heavily. Moreover, although you are protected by Moral Rights (see below), if the purchaser of the copyright were the rotten apple that every barrel contains, you might find that your work had been seriously mutilated and that you were not acknowledged as the author. Although in such a case you would have grounds on which to sue, it could prove to be very expensive and time-consuming, and there would be little reward at the end of it.

On the whole, publishers of books do not seek to purchase the copyright in them, but are content with a licence (see below). If a publisher tries to make you give up your copyright, you should stick up for your rights and do everything possible to avoid ceding your copyright. One exception, however, is the publication of plays for the amateur drama market by authors who are not eminent enough in the field to have the necessary clout to refuse the publisher's demand for the copyright. Fortunately, most play publishers are not dishonest and the author is unlikely to suffer at their hands.

The one instance in which it is common and acceptable practice for the author to surrender copyright is in respect of articles written for a reference book or encyclopædia, which is made up in whole or in part of contributions from a large number of different authors. The publishers of such books like to have the entire copyright under their control in order to protect it more easily, and also to avoid the complications of dividing a normal 10% royalty among dozens of contributors. However, a good publisher working on this basis will not only pay a fee at the time of accepting the article and purchasing the copyright, but will sign a commitment to pay additional sums each time the reference book or encyclopædia is reprinted or reissued in a revised edition.

Currently, there are two areas in which you may have to fight to retain your copyright – newspapers and magazines, and radio. Although you would normally offer a newspaper or magazine First British Serial Rights (see below), some magazines and newspapers will attempt to obtain copyright. One group of magazines when sending payment often asks the author to endorse the cheque on the back where there is a printed statement granting the magazine copyright in the article or story concerned. Do not sign, but strike the statement out (the cheque will not bounce just because you have done that). Recently a national newspaper announced that freelance writers would be expected to grant the paper copyright in any material it purchased from them; fortunately, after much protest, it was forced to climb down. The BBC has recently tried to claim copyright in broadcast talks and features, and the Freelance Consortium, made up of the Society of Authors, the Writers' Guild, BECTU (the Broadcasting, Entertainment, Cinematograph and Theatre Union) and the NUJ, is fighting vigorously to defend the copyright of the authors concerned.

Television has its own rules, and the ITV companies buy the copyright in scripts as a matter of course.

You should always be on the lookout for attempts to steal your copyright. Don't be afraid to fight for it – if needed, you will find good support from the various associations for writers (provided, of course, that you are a paid-up member).

It should be made clear that if you are employed as a writer (as for instance a journalist on the payroll of a newspaper), everything that you write for your employers is their copyright, not yours. Some employers have tried to insist that anything written by their employees out of office hours and which is not a part of their duties should nevertheless be regarded as the employers' copyright. Any such attempt can usually be successfully challenged by the author, unless perhaps the out-of-office work is too similar to that for which the employer pays, or which is based on material gathered in the course of the job.

Protecting your copyright

In most circumstances it is not necessary to do anything to protect your copyright. Publishers and other users of your material are normally as eager as you are to make sure that the copyright is not infringed. Some authors, convinced that their ideas will be stolen, go to great lengths to protect their work, sending themselves copies of their work in sealed and registered packages which they keep unopened so that they will be able to prove that the work had been completed by the date of posting, or putting a copy in the bank, with a dated receipt. I can only say that publishers do not normally steal ideas, and that no professional authors that I know go to these lengths. And if you do think that your idea has been stolen, you should remember that there are thousands upon thousands of writers out there, so it is not surprising if a few of them have the same brilliant inspiration at the same time. As Rosemary Horstmann points out in her book, *Writing for Radio*, there is a 'climate of ideas', when the same theme seems to be in the air at a certain time and is apparently picked up by the antennae of several authors more or less simultaneously.

In the past many writers have been particularly worried, and with some justification, about their ideas being pinched by radio and television companies. The Society of Authors, the Writers' Guild, the NUJ, the Musicians' Union, BECTU, the Directors Guild, Women in Film and Television, PACT (the Producers' Alliance of Cinema and Television) and the Scottish Independent Radio Producers Association together form the Alliance for the Protection of Copyright. In 1999 the Alliance produced a Code of Conduct which will go a long way towards eliminating the theft of copyright material, and which has been signed by the BBC, ITV, Channels 4 and 5 and the council of PACT.

In any case, before you cry, 'Stop, thief!', you should be aware that there is no copyright in ideas, which means you will still need to be absolutely certain of the close similarity between the details of your *development* of an idea and the programme which you think is based very closely on it, before you can take any action. Nor, by the way, is there copyright in titles.

It is not now necessary to put a copyright notice on your type-script, since nearly all the countries in which your work might be published are signatories of the Berne Convention, an international agreement which protects authors' copyright without any formalities. As for those countries which are not signatories of Berne, if anyone wants to publish or perform your work illegally, no amount of copyright notices is likely to stop them.

However, it does no harm, and may make you feel a little more secure, to add a copyright notice to your script. This will normally be in the form 'Copyright © Your Name' or '© Your Name' followed by the year in which it was written. If the work is published, it is virtually certain that a copyright notice will be included in the preliminary pages of the book, for although publishers know that it is not a legal requirement, they believe that it may put off anyone who thinks of infringing the copyright. The year shown in such a notice will be that of publication.

On the other hand, magazines and newspapers rarely carry any copyright notice, although you will sometimes see a formula such as that used by the Society of Authors in their journal *The Author*, which says '© The Society of Authors & contributors' and the year of publication. In the case of a magazine which carries a copyright notice in its own name, but makes no reference to the contributors, it is difficult to know the situation as far as the contributors are concerned; it could be that they have assigned their copyright to the magazine, or on the other hand that they in fact have retained their copyrights, and the magazine is lumping them in with its staff writers in a general form of protection.

Licences

When you sell your book to a publisher or to radio or television companies or to a theatre management, you will sign an agreement or contract. In this document you do not assign the copyright to the other party, but you do grant a licence to publish or broadcast or produce the work, and the contract will define (and limit) the rights which the purchaser may exercise, the territories in which the licence will be operative, the language (English, or other), and the period of time for which it will be effective.

The rights which the purchaser may exercise in respect of a book are usually known as Volume Rights, and in most cases this term covers the right of the publisher to produce hardback and paperback editions of the work or to license others to do so. The agreement will probably also cover a number of subsidiary rights, allowing the publisher to sell US or foreign rights, serial, digest, quotation and other rights. However, an agent, if you have one, will normally retain many of these rights, rather than giving them to the publisher, and will then attempt to sell them on your behalf. Incidentally, you do not need to put the words 'Volume Rights Only' on the typescript of a book – the publisher will take it for granted that this is what you are offering. However, if you have already sold US rights in the book, you should indicate to the British publisher that you are offering rights only to the British market.

For broadcasting, the rights which the purchaser may exercise are basically the first broadcast of the material and repeats.

For the stage, the contract will probably cover only the first production, the rights to subsequent productions being held by you or by an agent, while if your play is likely to be put on by amateurs, you will be able to sign an agreement with one of the play publishers, allowing them to print and publish copies of the play and to license, and collect fees from, amateur groups.

The territories granted in the licence will usually be specified as either British Commonwealth rights or World rights. A separate sheet is often attached to the contract listing all the territories in which the licence applies. If you have an agent, it is likely that he or she will wish to limit the licence of a British publisher or theatre management to the UK and the Commonwealth, and may even wish to exclude Australia or some of the other countries which would normally be considered to be part of that market, in order to make separate deals in those territories.

As for the language, the contract may be limited to publication or broadcast only in the English language (usually when an agent is involved), or may make no mention at all of such a restriction in which case the licensee will be able to sub-license foreign language editions or broadcasts.

Finally, the period for which the licence will be effective is usually the period of copyright, which means that it will continue in force until seventy years after the author's death. This is not as binding as it may sound if the contract also includes, as it should, a clause defining the circumstances in which the rights will revert to the author. However, some publishers may be willing for the licence period to be limited to twenty, or even ten years, after which it may be extended if the author and the publishers so wish, and if terms can be agreed between them. Alternatively, while the publishers retain the work for the period originally agreed, it is sometimes arranged that every ten years, or every twenty years, assuming that the book is continuing to sell, the contract shall be re-examined in order to alter various terms in it.

Moral rights

The Copyright, Designs and Patents Act of 1988 gave authors (and the directors of copyright films) four forms of protection known as Moral Rights. One of them protects authors from having someone else's work attributed to them, and another forbids the publication of a film or photograph commissioned from a photographer for private or domestic use. The two Moral Rights which are of greater interest to the majority of authors are known as the Right of Integrity and the Right of Paternity.

The Right of Integrity protects you against any derogatory treatment (i.e. any unauthorised mutilation or distortion) of your work in any adaptation or other treatment of it.

The Right of Paternity ensures that you will always be identified as the author of the work concerned, whether it is published in full or in part. However, for some reason known only to the legislators, the Right of Paternity, unlike the other Moral Rights, is not effective unless a notice is printed in the first edition of the work 'asserting' the right. This is usually in the form: 'The right of A. N. Author to be identified as the author of this work has been asserted by him/her in accordance with the Copyright, Designs and Patents Act 1988'.

Moral Rights do not apply to work published in a newspaper or magazine, and they are not, unlike copyright, assignable.

Serial rights

To most people the term 'serial' means a series of extracts from a longer work published in a newspaper or magazine, or a television or radio drama split into a number of parts, or indeed into daily instalments. In the world of publishing, however, 'serial' sometimes has a specialised meaning, becoming another term for a newspaper or magazine – a publication which appears regularly. Therefore, if you put First British Serial Rights or F.B.S.R. on the work that you submit to a newspaper or magazine, you are not suggesting your work is to be published in instalments. The wording is not relevant to the typescript of a book or play or other material for broadcasting.

Strictly, the wording First British Serial Rights should now be supplanted by First European Union Serial Rights. However, the old form is still used and is generally understood to mean material written in English.

Forgetting the complications, what you are saying is, most importantly, that you are offering the newspaper or magazine the right to publish the material once only and that you are retaining the copyright; secondly, you are testifying that the work has not been previously published. In fact, you do not need at present to put the F.B.S.R. mantra on work submitted to a newspaper – it will be taken for granted that that is what you are offering. However, you need to keep watching in case any newspaper or group of newspapers starts trying to steal the copyright from freelance contributors; if that happens, it will be wise to use the formula.

The only time it is really required is for submission to magazines, when you want to make it clear firstly that the rights offered are for this country only, leaving you free to offer First United States Serial Rights or First Australian Serial Rights or First South African Serial Rights to magazines in those countries. You are also saying that you are offering the piece for publication for the first time and for publication once only. You would then be free to sell the same piece again in the same territories, but this time as Second Serial Rights. Should you be able to sell it for a third or fourth or nineteenth time, those are all Second Serial Rights. It seems confusing at first but you will get used to the two ideas that in this context Serial doesn't mean what it sounds like and Second means any publication subsequent to the first.

Why should it be necessary to put First British Serial Rights on your work when you sell it to a magazine, and not normally when you are selling to a newspaper? Simply because certain publishers of magazines will otherwise take, or attempt to take, the copyright, and will then pass on the rights to other magazines within their group, especially in overseas publications, and your material will then be re-used without any further payment being made to you. Most magazines, like the newspapers, do not expect to acquire the copyright, but you have to guard yourself against those who will try. Incidentally, the 'baddies' usually give in quite readily when you make it clear that you are not falling for their blandishments and are retaining your copyright.

It is comparatively unlikely that you will sell Second Serial Rights in a short story, or indeed in features written for magazines, since these publications are usually distributed nationwide. On the other hand, if you write a feature for your local newspaper, you may well be able to sell it to other local newspapers in different parts of the country – the editors concerned will not mind, because their readerships do not overlap. You will in fact be syndicating your work, and you should inform the paper to which you submit of that fact. You can, if you wish, find agencies which will syndicate your work for you, but their commission is usually quite high.

Another possibility is that you might sell a collection of your stories or features, which have previously appeared in magazines or newspapers, to book publishers. You will be selling Volume Rights rather than Second Serial Rights. The book should contain a full list of the contents, giving details of the periodicals in which they were first printed and the dates of first publication.

Contracts

General

It is worth remembering that a contract is a binding legal document, whatever form it takes. One normally thinks of a contract as a typed or printed document containing a great many clauses couched in the kind of language that lawyers use. From a large publishing company, that is what you will get (and the larger the company, very often the longer and less comprehensible to anyone other than lawyers the contract is). However, a simple letter agreeing to print your work in a small magazine is, in legal terms, an enforceable contract, and this is also true of recorded speech, or an e-mail or other electronic means of communication.

The provisions of any contract must be strictly adhered to, by both parties. You are entitled to complain if the purchaser of the rights in your work does not keep to the contractual obligations; you must ensure that there is no respect in which you fail.

One of the most important parts of the contract is the Warranty Clause, in which you testify that you have the right to sign the contract, that the work is original to you, that you have not infringed anyone else's rights and that your material contains nothing illegal or offensive.

If you are aware of anything which may offend against this or any other clause (for instance, if you are writing about real-life people or putting them, slightly disguised, into a work of fiction, which might be libellous, or if you are going to be late in delivering your work), tell the purchaser immediately – a solution to the problem can usually be found.

Features and short stories in newspapers and magazines

Formal contracts are not normally exchanged between authors and the proprietors of newspapers and magazines. You can, instead, expect to have a letter setting out the details of the arrangement, that is to say the title, theme and length of a commissioned work, or simply the name of the piece if it is already written, plus the fee which will be paid. It is not usual for the purchaser to include a commitment as to when the piece will be published, although you may be given some idea if you speak to the editor concerned. In some cases the newspaper or magazine will attempt to do the entire deal orally. You should resist this and always get something in writing. As has already been made clear, if you are selling your work to a magazine you need to be sure that they are buying no more than First British Serial Rights (or First Serial Rights in whatever country the magazine is published in, or First European Serial Rights), while you do not need to bother about this if you are selling to a newspaper.

Books

A publishers' contract is usually a long and complex document. It will contain not only the definitions of the rights licensed to the publishers, the territories, languages and time period during which they may be used, but a great many other clauses covering the moneys to be paid to the author in the form of an advance and royalties and shares of subsidiary rights, the warranty in which the author guarantees that the work is original and does not contain anything libellous or of an illicit nature, the circumstances in which the agreement will terminate and the rights will revert to the author. The terms offered by different publishers can vary to a major extent, and there is no such thing as a standard contract, because even within one publishing house the contract offered to Author A is quite likely to differ from that presented to Author B.

Some years ago, the Society of Authors and the Writers' Guild drew up a basic contract which would be fair to authors. It is known as the Minimum Terms Agreement (MTA). It is not signed between individual authors and their publishers, but between the Society and the Guild on the one hand and individual publishing houses on the other. Under the agreement the publishing house commits itself to offering to members of the Society or the Guild terms which are not less favourable than those specified. Although MTAs have been signed with comparatively few publishers and their benefits are supposedly confined to Society and Guild members, the majority of publishers nowadays accept many of the terms even if they have not signed an MTA; they are prepared to offer such contracts to all authors, whether or not they are members of the Society or the Guild.

Not all the MTAs which have been signed are identical – the publisher signatories have in every case asked for certain amendments – but the contents of all are basically similar.

The MTA is not solely about money but also about the relationship of the author and the publisher, allowing the former the right to much more information and consultation than was the habit before the MTA was first drawn up. The more important, innovative and radical of these provisions come under four headings: Delivery and Acceptance, Production and Publication, Licence, and Option.

Delivery and acceptance
The MTA suggests that the contract should give a date by which the author is to deliver the typescript and details of the content of the book, if it has not already been completed. If the work is commissioned, it should conform to a reasonable extent with the description in the contract and should be of a standard which might reasonably be expected. If the publishers should require changes to be made, or should wish to reject the work, the author should be so informed within 30 days of delivery. Within a further 30 days the publishers should specify exactly what needs to be done or provide detailed reasons for the rejection. If the author should fail to deliver by the due date (or by some later date agreed with the publishers), should fail or be unwilling to make the changes for which the publishers ask, or because of a breach of the warranty clause (see page 43), the contract could be cancelled. The author, to whom all rights revert, could be asked to return any advance paid. However, if the publishers should reject the book for any other reason, they must pay the author the whole advance, including any part of it which has not previously been paid. Again, all rights would revert to the author.

Production and publication
The MTA constrains the publishers to consult the author about the publication date and to publish the work within 12 months of delivery of the final typescript (unless there are valid pro-gramming or other reasons for later publication).

All details as to the manner of production should be under the control of the publishers who will undertake to produce the book to a high standard. The publishers should consult the author and obtain his/her approval regarding the final number and type of illustrations. No changes in the title or text (apart from changes to make the work conform to the publishers' house style) should be made by the publishers without the author's consent, and indeed the publishers must obtain the author's approval of the finally edited text before it is sent to the printer. The author should be shown designers' roughs (or, if that is impracticable, proofs) of the jacket and should be fully consulted about the jacket and about the blurb in good time before publication, but the final decisions would be the publishers'.

The contract should include details of the format in which the book is to appear and the publishers' intended list price and initial print quantity, but since contracts are usually signed a long time before publication and all kinds of changes may occur, these will not be binding commitments. (Once such details are settled the publisher should, on request, inform the author of the number of copies of the work to be printed for the first and any subsequent printings.)

No changes of imprint (see page 21) or assignment of rights by the publishers should be made without the author's consent.

Licence

The Licence clause states that, while the copyright in the work remains the property of the author, the publisher shall be granted volume and/or other rights; it also lists the areas of the world and languages in which the publisher may publish the work, and specifies the period for which the licence is operative. A change in the wording of this last detail is the most controversial aspect of the MTA. In the past, it was the norm for publishers to be granted a licence for the period of copyright in the work (i.e. 50 years, or more recently 70 years, after the author's death). The MTA suggests that the licence period should initially be restricted to a twenty-year period from the date of first publication. On the tenth anniversary of the publication date either party may give written notice to the other that it wishes specified terms of the contract to be reviewed, and possibly altered in the light of comparable terms then prevailing in the trade. An additional section of the clause states that the author shall be given the opportunity to suggest that changes should be made to the contract if the term of the licence is to be renewed after the initial twenty-year period. These two proposals allow an author to enjoy the continuing success of the work to a greater extent than would have been the case in the past. If, when the time comes for the revision of the contract, the author has received an offer for the re-publication of the work from any other publishers, the initial publishers shall have the opportunity of matching the terms offered, but the author shall have the right to make the final decision. Not surprisingly, the publishers who have signed an

MTA with the Society of Authors and the Writers' Guild have not all been willing to accept such alterations of the standard modus operandi. However, it is always worthwhile to ask for the Licence clause to be in line with the MTA.

The Licence clause also demands that the publishers should inform the author of all sub-licences granted and should give him/her an opportunity to discuss all proposed major sub-licences, including First Serial (published in a newspaper or magazine prior to publication in book form), Second Serial (published in a newspaper or magazine after publication in book form), paperback, bookclub, US, film, television and merchandising deals. This clause, like all those in the MTA which give the author the right to be consulted or which say that the publishers may not act in certain matters without the author's approval, also includes, neither surprisingly or unfairly, a proviso that the author should neither delay giving approval nor withhold consent without reasonable cause.

Option
The Society of Authors and the Writers' Guild are both strongly opposed to any form of option which ties the author too closely to the publisher concerned, especially if it specifies the terms on which a second book may be signed up. Instead, the MTA suggests that the publishers may ask the author for first refusal on his/her next work, and must make an offer for it within three weeks of receipt of a synopsis or within six weeks of receipt of a completed work.

It should be noted that the MTA does not apply to: illustrated books in which the proportion of space taken up by illustrations is 40% or more; specialist works on the visual arts in which the proportion of space taken up by illustrations is 25% or more; books involving three or more participants in the royalties; technical books, manuals and reference works.

If you receive a contract from publishers, measure its provisions concerning delivery and acceptance, production and publication, options, and licence against the details printed above, clause by clause. Make sure that the licence is clear in respect of the rights, territories, language and period granted. Make sure, too, that the contract includes a specified publication date (not, for instance, anything as vague as 'within a reasonable period'), a clause guaranteeing to print a copyright notice in your name (although not essential, it will offer some protection against infringement) and your assertion of your Moral Right of Paternity, and a clear definition of the circumstances in which the agreement will terminate. You should not accept that the publishers may reject your book without giving detailed reasons and allowing you the chance of amending it, or that editorial changes could be made to the book without your approval. There should be no option clause committing you to giving the publishers the right to buy your next book on specific terms, especially not on exactly similar terms to those in the present contract (the terms should always be negotiable). Make sure that any rights not specified in the contract are reserved by you – new methods of presenting the original written word are developed so quickly and frequently these days that there is no knowing what may come. To reserve rights does not necessarily suggest that you will want to handle them yourself (you may be happy to give control to the publishers), but it does mean that the split of any proceeds must be negotiated at the time.

(See Chapter 5 for a summary and discussion of the financial terms proposed by the MTA.)

Poetry
If you succeed in selling a volume of poetry to a book publisher, all the details given in the Books section above will apply. If you are selling to one of the small poetry presses, the situation is in virtually every respect similar to that when you sell work to a magazine or newspaper.

Plays for the theatre
The Writers' Guild has negotiated agreements with both the Independent Theatre Council (ITC) and the Theatrical Management Association (TMA), which cover between them all the theatres in Great Britain and Northern Ireland, except for the English Stage Company, the Royal National Theatre and the Royal Shakespeare Company, and, in the case of ITC, the West End of London.

Both the ITC and TMA agreements are effective whether the play has been commissioned or is an existing script which has not been performed. The two agreements also include a similar, but not identical, clause regarding the period of the licence which the playwright grants to the management. In the ITC agreement the period is twelve months from the date of the first performance and for TMA nine months from the date of the first performance. Both also contain a warranty from the playwright that the work is original to him/her and contains no defamatory matter, and wording to protect the playwright's copyright and moral rights. There are also clauses covering the procedures to be followed if the management requires alterations to the script, the playwright's right to attend rehearsals and to be paid for doing so, and the free tickets which the playwright may be given for performances of the play.

The rights granted in these agreements are restricted to performances of the play in a theatre or theatres. They are not concerned with adaptations for film or television, or with publication rights, although they allow for the management to receive a percentage of the playwright's income from the play after his/her total earnings from it have exceeded a set sum.

The TMA agreement also sets out the different payments which the playwright shall receive in return for granting the management a licence to present or allow others to present the play in theatres in the UK, the West End of London, the USA or elsewhere in the world.

When selling the publication rights in a play, many of the provisions of the MTA will be included in the contract, but the publisher will also have the right to license performances of the play by amateur companies, and by professionals if licensing rights have not already been granted to the management which presented the play originally.

Films and television

If you have written and had published a work which subsequently is to be made into a film (whether for the cinema or for television), this is a case when you will have to grant the film company copyright in the script of the film and in further uses of it, but you will retain the remaining copyright in the work. This means that you will still own the copyright of the work throughout the world in every form other than film rights. The normal procedure begins with the purchase by the film company of an exclusive option to buy the film rights in the book. The company will not necessarily exercise the option but until it does (which frequently doesn't happen), the rights remain in your possession, except, of course, that you can't sell them elsewhere until the company releases you from the option. If the film company decides to go ahead, it may be agreed that you adapt your book for the screen, but this is unlikely unless you already have considerable experience in such work. Whether the script is written by you or another writer, the copyright in it will belong to the film company.

On the other hand, if the work is originally written as a film script, a film company will probably purchase the copyright in the entire work, and it will therefore be able itself to sell various rights, such as dramatisation for the stage or novelisation.

In either case, the company making the film will require complete assurances from you to the effect that you have not infringed any copyrights and that the work is completely free of defamatory material.

Basically, the same situation applies in the case of material written for television. The BBC's basic contract normally takes world television rights, which allows a complete broadcast of the work, or abridgements or translations of it, and includes repeat broadcasts, all subject of course to the payment of the appropriate fees. The author is usually able to retain all other rights, such as all publication rights throughout the world.

If the work has already been published in book form and a film is to be produced for television or for the cinema, the negotiations will probably be handled by the publishers concerned. You will get your share of the spoils as detailed in the publishing contract.

Radio

If you write and sell material to the BBC or to an independent station or group, you will simply grant radio rights to the organisation concerned. In most cases the contract will give the purchasing company the right to use the work throughout the world in the English language, with provision for repeats.

If the material has been published previously, it is again likely that the sale of rights will be handled by whoever purchased them in the first place. You will get your share of the royalties or purchase price in the proportions agreed in the original contract.

You should beware of an 'All Radio Rights' contract – an ARR agreement allows the company to broadcast the material as many times as it likes without the payment of repeat fees. Although such an agreement usually applies only in the case of very short items of an ephemeral nature and the author can use the work in other media, it amounts to giving away part of your copyright, which should always be avoided if possible.

Electronic rights

If you are signing a contract with a company which intends to exploit the electronic rights in your work, the agreement should contain clauses protecting your copyright and your Moral Rights, and should also set out what your royalties will be (they should normally rise to higher levels than those for books), when payments will be made to you, conditions for termination of the contract and so on – the basic contents of any acceptable agreement. They should grant the purchasing company only the electronic rights and preferably only those which the company is going to use; there should be no ambiguity in this clause, especially since new areas in electronic publishing may be developed, and you should make certain that the contract states clearly that all rights other than those specifically granted in the agreement are retained by you.

5. Income from the Sale of Your Work

As has already been indicated in Chapter 1, writing is not a particularly lucrative profession, unless you manage to establish yourself as a 'big name'. Is this because publishers and managers are mean? Well, yes, probably – but they have to be. They work in high-risk and extremely competitive industries; in order to be more generous to authors they would need to price their goods at a rate well beyond what the market will bear. Unfortunately, books, films, plays, television, radio, the Internet, magazines and newspapers are all luxuries when compared with essentials like food and clothing, and the man and woman in the street think of most of them as expensive.

But, looking particularly at books, you may wonder about all the price cuts that we have seen since the Net Book Agreement was abolished. How do publishers manage to reduce prices in those instances? Shouldn't all books be cheaper and wouldn't they sell better if they were? If you look carefully you will see that in almost every case the books concerned are bestsellers or near-bestsellers. The publisher, the bookseller and the author all take cuts in the moneys they would expect to earn on such titles, and can afford to do so because they rely on large initial print quantities, bulk orders from bookshops and enthusiastic buying by the general public. An increased number sold at a lower rate of profit has to make up for the loss of a more substantial profit per book. As for cutting the price on all books in order to create more sales, the cut would have to be substantial to have any real effect and, once you move away from the bestseller, the net profit margins just do not allow of any such exercise.

And there has to be a reasonable profit on at least most of the titles on a publishers' list. Publishers are in business to make money to pay their staffs and their overheads and to be able to invest in future projects, and increasingly nowadays to make money for their shareholders. As a great publisher, Sir Stanley Unwin, said, 'The publisher's first duty to his authors is to remain solvent' – a maxim which of course applies to those involved in other forms of the written word than books.

Suitably chastened after the little homily above, you will perhaps nevertheless wish to know what, as a minimum, you are likely to earn, and in the case of royalties, what percentages you may expect. Contracts are so complex nowadays that even experienced authors need the services of an agent or of the Society of Authors, the Writers' Guild, the NUJ or similar organisations to make sure that the contracts they sign are fair. But at least this book can try to give some guidance.

You should be aware that there is no uniformity in the rewards for authors in any of the media connected with the written word, so we shall be talking of figures which are likely to be in general use in the various industries, but to which there may be exceptions. Additionally, agreements with purchasing organisations such as the BBC, theatre managements, and so on, are periodically renegotiated, so that while the remunerations shown in this chapter were valid at the time of writing (late Autumn 1999 and the first weeks of 2000), there may have been changes since.

Newspapers and magazines

If you want to get into print, the easiest way of doing so, apart from writing something of outstanding brilliance, is probably to target newspapers and magazines. You do not need to be a member of the National Union of Journalists, or any other union, to have your work accepted and, indeed, most magazines, although they have the regular features written by staff members, are dependent on freelances to fill their pages.

How much will you get for your work? The NUJ recommends suitable minimum fees for freelances, and the current figures are as follows: for magazines, depending on the size of the circulation and the advertising rates, between £160 and £400 per 1000 words; for national newspapers, £210 per thousand words; for regional and provincial newspapers (calculated on the basis of 'lines', usually consisting of four words per line), £2 for up to and including 10 lines (which would cover most fillers), and 20p for each additional line.

These figures are for guidance only, since there is great variation in what different newspapers and magazines pay; moreover, they are likely to be top-of-the-range prices, especially if you are a beginner. The NUJ quite rightly suggests that you should fight to get their recommended rates, or something approaching them quite closely, but until you are established you may have to settle for far less. Some specialist magazines, with a small circulation, will never pay more than a pittance. However, once you have become a regular contributor to a newspaper or magazine you are likely to be rewarded with higher payments (and should ask for them if they are not volunteered) than you would get as a beginner and, if in due course you are recognised as a big name, you will be able to dictate your own terms. In the meantime, the stories or features (the term which in the trade is preferred to 'articles'), though poorly paid, may help to establish your reputation in other spheres and so increase your sales.

The NUJ's *Freelance Fees Guide*, which they will send on request, deals with rates for many other kinds of work, such as editing, photography, illustrations and design, in addition to features and stories.

Payment for work published in a newspaper or magazine is a one-time sum, so no royalties are involved. The money should reach you on publication, but will very often not be sent automatically, but only in response to an invoice from you when the piece appears in print. Many newspapers and magazines do not notify contributors that their work has actually been used, and you have to keep an eye on the issues of the publication in question.

Whether your work is commissioned or simply accepted when you submit it, it is strongly advisable to get the commission or the acceptance in writing.

Short stories

The rates of payment for short stories are similar to those for journalism, that is to say, between £160 and £400 per thousand words. However, some magazines are more generous than others, and some are much meaner. Again, if you are a beginner you are likely to be poorly rewarded, but can expect better payment as you become established.

Books

The Society of Authors and the Writers' Guild have together tried to lay down a basic contract which would be fair to authors. It is known as the Minimum Terms Agreement (MTA), and some details of how it works have been given in Chapter 4.

54

As has already been described, the MTA is concerned in part with the relationship between author and publishers, and the need for an author to be considered as a partner in the publication of a book. The MTA also, of course, suggests minimum financial terms. We can look at them under five main headings: advance, royalties, subsidiary rights (in which, although they are usually treated separately, I include US, translation and bookclub rights), remainders and accounts.

Advance

Regular publishers normally pay an advance against royalties and other income likely from the sale of copies of the book and of subsidiary rights. The advance, which in most cases is non-returnable unless the author reneges on the contract in some way, is in fact a down payment against the book's earnings. You will, therefore, not receive any further payment from the publisher until the amount of the advance is exceeded by the royalties earned on sales of the work, plus your share of any other income generated by the book. The amount of the advance offered by the publisher is usually calculated as a proportion of the sum which the book is expected to earn over a period of time or from the sale of the first printing. You may expect the advance to be paid in two or three tranches – part on signature of the agreement, part on delivery and/or acceptance of the typescript and part on publication – but there are no set rules about this. The method may vary from one publishing house to another and, occasionally, according to your own financial requirements.

As for the size of the advance, prepare to be disappointed. There is no trade-wide agreement on this point such as exists in the theatre and radio and television. The reason for this is that every book is different in so many ways – in length, typesize, number of illustrations, print quantity, retail price, etc., whereas plays and material for radio and TV can at least always be measured in the length of time they occupy. The MTA does not specify any minimum amount, but specifies that the advance should be 65% of the author's expected earnings on sales of the first printing if the publisher is bringing the book out only in hardback or only in paperback, or 55% if the book will appear in both formats.

Any publisher will tell you that the firm's profits are invariably adversely affected by unearned advances – that is to say, when the advance paid is more than the book earns from sales of copies and of rights. Consequently, publishers regularly try to keep the advance to a minimum. For a first book you will be doing quite well if your advance is in four figures, and even a well-established writer may find great difficulty in pushing the publisher into an advance of £10,000 or more. Write a book which the publisher believes will be a bestseller, and the advance will not disappoint you; write a whole string of bestsellers and you will be a millionaire; write something which is just another book, and you might have enough to part-exchange your old computer for a new one.

There is a widespread belief that the amount of effort that publishers will put into selling a book is in direct proportion to the size of the advance. It is certainly true that publishers will work hardest for the book for which a fortune has been paid, but is it true for the books which are not in that class? Yes, but you have to understand that both the advance and the amount of publicity and promotion which the book will receive are calculated on the basis of the publishers' sales expectations. The run-of-the-mill books, with a comparatively small advance paid, will still get their share of attention – it simply does not pay publishers to neglect them.

You can always attempt to negotiate over the amount paid in advance and it is quite possible that you will be able to increase it by a few hundred pounds, but little more than that. It is only good business sense on the publisher's part to make an initial offer which leaves the firm with a little in hand in case the author (or the agent) wants to haggle, but it is not going to be a large amount, nor will it be out of line with the publisher's sales predictions for the book. And the increase will not affect the amount of effort that the publisher makes for the book in question.

If you have to accept a comparatively small advance, at least you will have the small consolation that earnings from your royalties may start much more quickly.

Royalties

Apart from such a basic matter as the publishers' commitment to publish your work, the most important parts of any publishing agreement, it seems to me, are the clauses dealing with royalties. This is because you must be sure that if your book keeps on selling after the advance has been earned you are taking in a reasonable share of the profits. It is fairly standard throughout the industry for the royalties on sales of a hardback book in the home market (i.e. the United Kingdom and the Irish Republic) to start at 10% of the publisher's recommended retail price. There should also be some provision for the rate to increase, after a given number of sales has been reached, to 12½% and eventually to 15% in the case of the hardback (the MTA recommends that these jumps should be after 2500 and 5000 sales respectively). There may be reduced royalties (perhaps four-fifths of the normal rate) on bulk sales of the work or sales at a discount of 50% or more. On overseas sales it is usual to calculate the royalties as a percentage of the price received by the publishers, and the MTA recommends 10% of the price received on the first 2500 copies, 12½% on the next 2500 copies and 15% thereafter. Royalties on books for children are customarily paid at a lower rate to take account of the cost of illustrations and the lower retail prices which the market demands.

Some publishers prefer to use a percentage of the price which they receive on the books they sell in the home market as well as on overseas sales. However, if the author is not to lose out on such an arrangement, the royalty percentage needs to start at a much higher level, such as 16% of the price received.

On paperbacks the normal starting royalty for sales in the home market is 7½% of the retail price, and the MTA suggests that this should rise to 10% after 40,000 copies have been sold. There may be a provision that only four-fifths of the royalty will be paid on sales at a discount of 52½% or more. The royalty on overseas sales is usually 6% of the British retail price. Again the royalties for children's books are at a lower level.

Subsidiary rights
Further moneys can come in from the sale of subsidiary rights. Some of these will be one-off sums for a single use of the work, while others will be on a royalty basis. It is impossible to give any indication of the amounts likely to be earned from these sales, but it can be considerable. The important thing is that the original contract should be drawn up so that the moneys are split fairly between the author and the publishers. The MTA recommends that the author should receive the following percentages (but it must be pointed out that the figures are negotiable, and many publishers will try to be somewhat less generous):

- Paperback rights sold to independent paperback publishers: 60%, rising at a point to be negotiated to 70%.
- Book club: on bound copies or sheets sold to the book club, 10% of the publishers' receipts, and on copies manufactured by the book club 60% of the publishers' receipts.
- If the publishers sell United States rights to American publishers who will produce an edition of the book, 80% if an agent is involved, and 85% in other cases. If the publishers sell bound copies of the British edition to American publishers, a royalty based on the US retail price. And if the American publishers buy sheets from the British house, 15% of the price received, unless the discount is 60% or more, when the royalty will reduce to 10%.
- Translation: 75% if an agent is involved (the publishers' percentage to include the agent's commission) and 80% otherwise.
- First serial, electronic, TV and radio dramatisation, film and dramatic, sound and video recording: 90% (most publishers will baulk at this, and suggest a 50/50 split, but that is really unacceptable and, although you may have to settle in the end for a lesser figure, 90% is not unreasonable).
- Second serial, strip cartoon, condensation rights for magazines, single-voice TV and radio readings, straight readings for audio/audio visual use, graphic novel: 75%.
- Anthology and quotation rights: 50% on licences of £100 or less, otherwise 60%.
- Condensation rights for books: 50%.
- Merchandising, one-shot periodical: 80%.
- Large print rights: 55%.
- Other hardback reprint rights: 60% (80% if publication is prior to or simultaneous with a paperback edition published under one of the publishers' own imprints).

It is important to see that a clause is included stating that reprographic rights will be handled for both author and publishers by the Authors' Licensing and Collecting Society and the Publishers' Licensing Society respectively. Any other income from reprography not covered by collective licensing schemes should be handled by the publishers and the income divided 50:50.

Equally essential is a clause stating that Public Lending Right and all other rights not specified in the rest of the contract are reserved by the author.

Remainders

Since remainders are usually sold by the publishers at a price below the cost of manufacture, it has been trade practice not to pay royalties on them. However, the MTA suggests that the author is entitled to a 5% royalty on the price received by the publishers. The author must, of course, also be permitted to purchase copies of the book at the remainder price or to be given them without charge if the publishers intend to destroy them.

Accounts

Royalty accounts should be prepared by the publishers twice a year and sent out, together with other moneys due to the author, within three months from the end of the sales period on which accounts are based. Some publishers pay royalties only annually, a practice which no author should accept without a serious struggle, unless the publishers can justify the practice.

Good agreements also contain a clause stating that any sum of £100 or more due to the author in respect of sub-licensed rights shall be paid to the author by the end of the month following receipt, provided that the advance has been earned.

If you receive a contract from a publisher, measure its financial provisions against the details printed above. While you may feel like accepting a certain amount of leeway in the terms, you should certainly question any of them which vary considerably. The publisher may not be willing to make any changes, but should at least accept that your queries are not unreasonable. Be wary of any attempt to specify particularly low royalties on the sale of heavily discounted books. In any case in which the figures in the publishers' contract vary considerably from those recommended in the MTA, fight hard to get an improvement. And finally, remember that the terms quoted above come from a *Minimum* Terms Agreement. Even if you are being published for the first time, it is just possible that you will be able to do better for yourself in this or that respect.

It should be noted that the MTA does not apply to: illustrated books in which the proportion of space taken up by illustrations is 40% or more; specialist works on the visual arts in which the proportion of space taken up by illustrations is 25% or more; books involving three or more participants in the royalties; technical books, manuals and reference works.

Poetry

The rewards for poets are scanty, unless you become recognised as a poet of substance, and even then you will be fortunate if you make a lot of money from your writing. Beginners will probably find it difficult to get published except in some of the so-called 'little magazines', and the payment for such publication is often a few free copies of the issue in which your poems appear (and a request for you to become a subscriber to the magazine). Fees for reading your poetry to an audience may remunerate you reasonably well if the event is part of a festival or something of that kind. The amount paid will vary according to your fame. If it is a matter of performance poetry in a pub, it will probably not be paid. Collections of poetry in book form by a single unknown writer are usually undertaken by commercial publishers only as a sop to their consciences and an indication that they are not totally Philistine, rather than in the hope of making any money. So the amount that you will receive in the form of an advance and royalties is likely to be minimal. However, anthologies are far more regularly published, and can often achieve high sales figures, so if you contrive to write a poem which the public at large takes to its collective heart, you may be able to pick up quite a sizeable amount from anthology fees.

A major outlet for poetry is the Internet. If you simply publish your work through one of the many websites devoted to poetry your poems will be read, but it is very unlikely that you will receive any financial benefit, and of course, anyone who is interested can simply download the material without any form of payment to you. On the other hand, if you have a 'slim volume' of your verse, you could create your own website, give your e-mail address, and invite those who visit the site to get in touch if they would like to purchase a copy of the book.

Plays for the theatre

The Writers' Guild has negotiated agreements with both the Independent Theatre Council (ITC) and the Theatrical Management Association (TMA), which cover between them all the theatres in Great Britain and Northern Ireland, except for those in the West End of London, the English Stage Company, the Royal National Theatre and the Royal Shakespeare Company.

The agreement with ITC lays down minimum payments for the licence to produce plays according to their length, as follows:

- for a play over 70 minutes   £5309.20
- or a play between 30 and 70 minutes   £3538.80
- or a play under 30 minutes   £1769.40

These strange amounts (and others to follow below) have come about because of increases calculated as a percentage of the previous figures, rather than by additions in round figures. The payments listed refer to the straight, non-returnable fee for a licence which is limited to a twelve-month period after the first performance of the play. A further fee is paid if the period is extended, £500 provided that the rights granted to the management continue to be exclusive, or £100 if the rights are non-exclusive. In addition, the playwright receives 8% of net box office receipts after the first £35,000, which goes to the management. If the play is produced elsewhere during the first five years after its première, the author agrees to pay the original management 8% of his earnings from the play as presented by the new management, after the first £20,000.

The agreement with the TMA differs considerably. Firstly, the sums payable to the playwright are based on the theatre in which the play is to be performed. The theatres which are party to this agreement are divided into three classes according to the rates paid to actors appearing in them, as agreed with Equity, the actors' union. Thus in the top theatres the relevant total fee is £6236, for the next grade £5046 and for the third level £4453. For a short play, these figures are halved, and if the play is one of a number of plays presented together, the sums are divided equally between the writers concerned. Further sums are payable to the author if the management, after the first presentation of the play, wishes to take up one or more of four specified options: the right to present the play (a) in the UK, except the West End of London, when the sum payable is £1853, (b) in the West End, £3089, (c) in the USA, £3089, and (d) in the rest of the English-speaking world (excluding South Africa) £2471.

Secondly, although all these sums are non-returnable, approximately 53% of them are a fee, while the remaining sum is an advance against royalties at a rate of 8% of the net box office receipts, without any commencing threshold.

Thirdly, if the playwright has received a total of £35,297 from the sale of film and audio rights, book publication rights (in English), merchandising rights, or the right granted to parties other than the management to present the play in English in the UK, the playwright must pay to the management a percentage of subsequent earnings dependent on how many performances of the play have been given under the management's auspices, as follows: 17–24 performances – 5%, 25–49 performances – 10%, 50 or more performances – 12½%.

In both agreements, no difference is made to the total amount payable as a fee or as an advance whether the play is commissioned or is already complete when the agreement is drawn up, but the tranches in which the moneys are paid vary. If the work has not been completed, the playwright will receive part of the amount on signature of the commissioning contract and a further part on delivery of the completed play; for the author of a completed play, the two sums are combined and paid on signature of the agreement.

Both agreements contain clauses which protect the author's copyright and moral rights, and the procedure to be followed when the management requires alterations to the script. The final version of the play must be approved by the author, and thereafter changes will not be allowed. The writer is also entitled to approve the casting of the play, to attend rehearsals (for which a daily fee and expenses will be paid), to be consulted regarding the contents of the programme and publicity material, and to receive complimentary tickets.

Whether the TMA or the ITC agreement is used, the playwright does not grant the management control of book publication rights. Plays are usually published by specialist houses and it is through them that the amateur market can be tapped. The publishers of the play sell copies of the play to the amateur groups who want to put the play on and charge them a fee for each performance. The playwright gets a royalty on the sale of the copies, usually 10%, and 50% of the performance fee. If the play is not too outré and has neither too few characters (in most cases, tickets for amateur productions are sold largely by the cast) nor too many parts for men, the royalties and fees can be very lucrative. It is also the amateurs who provide a market for one-act plays.

Professional companies who wish to present the full-length play will usually buy copies from the publisher, but the contract regarding their production will be arranged between the company and the playwright or, more frequently, his/her agent.

Radio

The fees paid by the BBC (which sets the standard for the radio broadcasting industry) are complex, because it all depends on whether you have written a play or some other piece for broadcasting, or have given a talk or have been interviewed, on whether you are a beginner or an experienced writer for radio, and on which service broadcasts the piece, and so on.

The fees, negotiated between the BBC and the various authors' societies and associations are as follows:

- For radio drama: £64.80 per minute for established writers, £42.57 per minute for beginners, with an attendance allowance of £38.12. A sum between 65% and 85% of these figures is used for dramatisations of existing works, depending on the amount of original material the writer has added.
- For features and documentaries the rate for professional broadcasters is £178.50 for up to 7 minutes, and £25.50 per minute thereafter.
- For Script and Read (i.e. you both write the piece and read it for broadcasting): for professionals £19.25 per minute, for non-professionals £10.40 per minute.
- For Script only: for professionals £15.00 per minute, for non-professionals £8.30 per minute.

If you interview someone, you will be paid £50.00 for up to 5 minutes, £55.00 for 5 to 8 minutes and £66.50 for 8 to 10 minutes. Additional sums are payable if you are undertaking further interviews linked to the first one. If you are employed as a reporter, the daily rate is £106.00.

If you are interviewed, you will be given £29.00 for up to 5 minutes, £35 for 5–8 minutes and £40 for 8 to 10 minutes. But while these figures apply to the five national channels, they are not applicable to local radio, whether the interview is broadcast by a BBC regional station or an independent. For whatever reason you are interviewed, the local radio channels will probably have to be cajoled into paying any fee at all. This is particularly true if you are given a few minutes on a chat show to talk about your new book, since they seem to believe that the publicity you get from being interviewed should be regarded as your fee.

Different fees are paid in respect of the reading of published work. On domestic radio: £12.52 per minute of a play or prose, £12.52 per half minute for poetry, £9.77 per minute for prose dramatisations and £8.34 per minute for prose translations. On the World Service in English, these rates are halved and for local radio may be reduced to 25% of the national rate. However, local rates are sometimes open to negotiation.

Repeat fees are normally 50% of the amount paid for the original broadcast.

Television

The Writers' Guild has an agreement with PACT (the Producers' Alliance of Cinema and Television), which provides for minimum payments to Guild members according to the type of production concerned, as follows:

- For a film budgeted at £750,000 or less, whether designed for the cinema or television: a minimum advance of £14,000. No extra sum is paid as an advance in respect of other uses of the film. The fees are reduced pro rata if the film runs for less than 90 minutes.
- For a film budgeted at from £750,000 to £2 million, whether designed for the cinema or television: the same minimum advance of £14,000, but a further £5000 is payable on account of additional sums varying between £1000 and £9750 for other uses of the film, including repeats. The fees are reduced pro rata if the film runs for less than 90 minutes.
- For a feature film budgeted at over £2 million: a minimum advance payment of £23,200, and a further £8000 on account of additional sums, varying between £1500 and £13,000, for use of the film, including repeats, on various television circuits throughout the world.
- For television series and serials in which the storyline has been supplied to the author: a minimum advance in respect of one transmission on a UK television channel of £5500 for a script lasting one hour or more, and pro rata for shorter works, with an additional £5500 if the management wishes to purchase world rights. Extra sums are payable on account of UK repeats and US first use and repeats.

The advances mentioned above are normally paid in the following stages: on commencement and on acceptance of the Treatment (a synopsis of the content of the proposed film), on commencement and on delivery of the First Draft (a full development of the treatment, with action and dialogue), on commencement and on delivery of the Second Draft (an amended version of the First Draft), and when Principal Photography (with a final, accepted script) begins.

While the PACT agreement refers to films, it is clearly intended primarily to cover material written for television.

The Guild also has agreements with the Independent Television Companies which lay down payments for Guild members varying according to whether the author has had a certain number of teleplays accepted, or is new to writing for television but has already established a reputation in other media, or is a complete newcomer. Different rates also apply to original teleplays, dramatisations and adaptations, and serials and series, and range from £1250 paid to an inexperienced writer who has been given the storyline for writing a script of not more than 20 minutes in running time as part of a serial, to almost £14,000 for an original teleplay by an established television writer. The agreements also cover fees, expressed in percentages, for showing the film on other networks than the one which commissioned the work, for repeats and for use in foreign countries.

The summaries above are necessarily shortened versions of the agreements between the Guild and PACT and the Guild and the Independent Television Companies, which also contain provisions regarding such matters as credits, the fees payable for attendance at rehearsals, alterations to the script, etc. The figures shown are valid for Guild members at the time of writing (late 1999 and early 2000). If you are writing for films or television it is not compulsory to join the Writers' Guild, but it is undoubtedly highly advisable, even if you have an agent, which is also desirable. An agent will cost you 10% or possibly 15% of your earnings and membership of the Guild is not cheap, so is it worth having both? Yes, because the agent should be able to find the right purchaser for your work, while Guild membership will ensure that you get the best terms and a good contract. There is the additional advantage that, for Guild members, PACT will contribute towards their Guild pension schemes.

The Writers' Guild also negotiates with BBC Television regarding fees paid for Television Drama; the current rates are:

	for an established writer	for a beginner
• for a 60 minute teleplay	£7170	£4551
• for a 50 minute series or serial	£5423	£3754
• for a 50 minute dramatisation	£3860	£2619
• for a 50 minute adaptation	£2313	£1579
• plus an attendance fee of £65 per day.		

A reading on television from an already published work is rewarded with a fee of £18.97 per minute for prose, and £22.02 per half minute for poetry.

Films

There are usually two contracts to be signed if a film company wants to make a motion picture, designed to be shown in cinemas rather than just on television, from a book or a play or other material which you have written. The first is an Option Agreement, under which you will be paid a negotiable fee, depending on your fame as a writer and the success of the material from which the film is to be made. The fee is non-returnable, so you keep it even if the company decides not to go ahead. As a rough guide, you can expect 10% of the final purchase price.

The second contract, the Purchase Agreement, is usually negotiated at the same time, and is attached to the option agreement as an exhibit. It is signed only when the company finally decides to make the film. At that stage, the writer's payment, which is usually quite substantial, may consist of a lump sum, less the option money, and a further lump sum when the cameras start to roll; alternatively, you may receive a smaller lump sum plus a share in the gross profits that the film earns. However, such an arrangement is not only comparatively unusual, but is rarely very rewarding, not simply because film-making is a gambling business, but because in some strange way films never make much of a gross profit by the time that the lawyers and accountants have played with the figures. So what about a share in net profits? Unless you are a world-famous author and are selling to a film company your worldwide bestseller, which has an immense and universal appeal, you are not likely to be offered a share of net profits. Even if you are, your share won't amount to much, if anything at all, since net profits are even more likely to disappear than the gross variety.

In fact, any writer's earnings are almost always restricted to the lump sums paid on the signing of the option and later of the final contract. The amounts of the earnings are tied to the film's budget, which is, of course, what you might think of as a movable feast. The rewards that the writer will earn from films (and for that matter teleplays) are just as unpredictable as those of the novelist or the playwright or anyone else who works with words.

If the film does exceptionally well, there may be substantial earnings through the exploitation of merchandising, although your share of such income is likely to be restricted to 30%.

Electronic rights

If you have a contract for the publication of your work in book form, it will almost certainly contain a clause specifying how any income from the sale of electronic rights should be divided (as already indicated, the publishers will want to share it 50/50, but you should ask for the split to be 90/10 in your favour – and should fight hard to get at least something of that order). On the other hand, if publishers working in the sphere of electronics – producing CD-ROMS, for instance – agree to publish in electronic form a book you have written, then you could expect an agreement fairly similar to that which you would sign with book publishers, except that it will convey only the electronic rights. It will preferably be restricted to the particular form of those rights which the publisher actively requires. The royalty in such a case would probably start at 15% of the receipts, but should rise to 25%, either in steps or in one giant stride, since the economics of the business are such that the publisher's costs diminish considerably once the initial work has been done.

The use of electronics, and especially the Internet, is increasing daily, and the experts tell us that all our business transactions and our leisure activities will soon be based on these modern marvels. They say, of course, that books will disappear – a fear which was uttered with equal pessimism when films, radio and television, in turn, first appeared. Well, we shall see. Quite recently a major publishing company, large enough to be a PLC and to be quoted on the London Stock Exchange, announced that it was to put all of its books on the World Wide Web, so that anyone who can surf the Net can download all the books on to a computer. The publishers are confident that they will sell even more books, because the Internet will generate interest in surfers who would not otherwise be aware of the books' existence, and as readers these people will prefer to have the material in bound book form rather than to download it as print-outs, which would certainly not be as convenient as a conventional book and might be more expensive.

Whatever developments the future brings, it is very clear that the possibilities in the use of electronics are growing daily. It is difficult to predict how authors will be rewarded, how long licences for the rights should last, how copyright will be protected and, indeed, what undreamt-of clauses will have to be inserted in any agreement that an author signs. Fortunately the Society of Authors, the Writers' Guild, the NUJ and other bodies who deal with the written and spoken words, plus all the competent literary agents, will be there to guide us.

Kill fees

If a newspaper or magazine accepts for publication something which you have written, but subsequently decides not to go ahead with it, you have a reasonable hope of getting what is known as a 'kill fee' – a payment which can be regarded as compensation not only for your disappointment but because, while the material has been in their pipeline, you have missed the opportunity of selling it elsewhere. Not all newspapers and magazines will pay a kill fee (although a threat of legal action may work if they are recalcitrant), and you will certainly have to ask for it, rather than expecting it to be offered automatically. You also need some firm written evidence of the initial acceptance.

On the whole, newspapers and magazines, not surprisingly, don't like having to pay kill fees, even though the fault is theirs, and the amount of money involved is not likely to be particularly handsome – something like 20% or 25% of the original agreed fee would probably be the norm, with 50% as an upper limit. Obviously, the fee paid depends to some extent on the circumstances and the specific reason for the newspaper or magazine reneging on its commitment. If it has gone out of business, unless it was part of a large group, you have little hope of any compensation. With payment of a kill fee all rights in the material revert to you immediately.

In the case of book publishers who, after accepting the book, decide not to go ahead with publication (which, among other reasons, can happen if the editor who accepted or commissioned your book leaves the company), your position is easier, because you should have a signed contract which sets out the publishers' commitment in clear terms. It is normal practice that in these circumstances, the publishers will pay the advance in full (or that part of it which has not yet been paid), and you will then be free to offer the book elsewhere, the rights having reverted to you. Some publishers try to make the condition that you should refund to them any sum you receive as an advance from another firm, up to the amount of the total advance that they (the reneging publishers) paid, but this is not an acceptable option, and should be firmly rejected by the author.

A brief reminder: kill fees are paid only if the work has been commissioned or accepted for publication or performance.

What if your work is published but you don't get your money?

This is often a major problem, especially since all the companies whose lifeblood is the written word in some form or other are in a high-risk business. Failures are common, especially in the case of small new magazines appealing to a highly specialised audience. But other more substantial magazines come and go, publishers collapse or sell out, theatres close, and television and radio are subject to arbitrary changes of programme content made by the controllers, while films depend on the raising of vast sums of money, which are not always available.

If your work is published or used in some way, but you do not get paid, you will probably have to grin and bear it if the company concerned has declared itself bankrupt, although it may be worth trying to get a claim in to the Official Receiver. In other cases, where the firm is still extant, if all your attempts to persuade the people who owe you money to stump up (and you should keep copies of all correspondence on the matter), you may find it helpful to go in the first place to your local Trading Standards Office, which is accustomed to chasing reluctant payers and extracting the money from them.

If that fails, your next option is to go to the County Court. This will be quite an expensive operation for you in terms of the time and the hassle involved, and if the amount owing is quite small, you may decide that it is best just to forget it. If you do want to continue with your claim, either because the money is important to you or as a matter of principle, you may be encouraged by the fact that recent amendments to the legal rules have simplified the procedures, and the costs involved. If you are claiming a sum in excess of £15,000 (this is known as a 'multi-track' case), you will certainly need the assistance of a solicitor because the case could be conducted in the High Court. If the claim is for between £5000 and £15,000 (a 'fast track' case) you may be able to conduct your own case in the County Court, but would certainly find professional legal advice to be helpful, especially in discovering exactly what you have to do to get the case in motion. If the amount claimed is less than £5000 (a 'small claims track' case), as the majority of unpaid sums are likely to be, the procedure is similar to that which, in the past, was used when making an application to the Small Claims Court.

Basically, you are required to fill in a claim form (Form N1, obtainable from any county court), stating the facts of the case, including a summary of the efforts you have made to obtain the due payment, and the amount of money claimed (you are entitled to charge interest from the day the payment became overdue). Send it, with a copy for each defendant and the relevant fee, to the Court Manager of your local county court. The court will then serve the claim on the defendant. What happens next depends on the defendant's reaction – it may produce the money for you, or the claim may be admitted in part only, or the claim may be disputed, or there may be no reply. Advice on how to proceed if the response is not satisfactory to you can be obtained from the offices of the county court, from a solicitor, from a Citizen's Advice Bureau, or from the Society of Authors or the Writers' Guild, if you are a member.

The next step may be a small claims hearing, when the case will be decided by a district judge. If the verdict is in your favour, the defendant may pay up without further ado. If you do not get your money, the defendant is in real trouble, and the bailiffs will be sent in to obtain a cheque or, if that fails, to seize property in lieu of the cash owing (but it has to be said that bailiffs are not always successful in getting redress for you, especially from defendants who are experienced in dodging them).

As a nation, we are becoming increasingly litigious, following the example from our cousins across the Atlantic, but it is still wise to avoid, if you can, having to resort to the law. Unless you feel strongly about the principle involved, or the sum of money is itself important to you, it is quite good advice simply to write the debt off to experience and to get on with your next piece of work.

6. Sources of Additional Income

Public Lending Right

Ever since the establishment of the Public Library system in Britain, authors have felt it unfair that they should receive no more than a single royalty on the copy of a book which would be taken out and read by borrower after borrower. Following a long campaign in the 1970s, led by Brigid Brophy and Maureen Duffy of the Writers' Action Group, and supported by the Society of Authors and the Writers' Guild, a law granting authors the right to receive payment for the borrowing of their books from Public Libraries was finally passed in 1979. It took a further three years to set up what was necessarily an extremely complicated recording system. The first distribution of moneys, covering borrowings for the twelve months ended June 30th, 1983, did not take place until early in 1984.

Public Lending Right (PLR) is Government funded. It is not a concession, or a privilege, but a right, enshrined in law, that belongs solely to the author. Moneys received under PLR are not shared with publishers, nor with literary agents, unless the author asks the publisher or agent to collect any amounts due, in which case a commission is naturally taken.

The PLR scheme is administered by the Registrar (currently Dr Jim Parker) and his staff. The borrowing figures are compiled by recording all borrowings in a twelve-month period from a varying selection of Public Libraries up and down the country, in both urban and country districts. The resultant figures are then used to extrapolate a notional countrywide total for each book. The procedure is much more complex than that may sound, and every effort is made to produce results which are balanced and fair.

The payment per borrowing is small (currently 2.18p) and, even though the figures used represent all loans throughout the UK, the amounts which the majority of authors receive will certainly not make the difference between penury and riches.

Currently, out of 27,000 authors who have registered for PLR, approximately 35 per cent of them receive nothing (no payment is made until an author's PLR earnings reach a minimum of £5), and 44 per cent receive between £5 and £100. On the other hand, about 130 of the more popular authors receive between £5000 and £6000, the latter figure being the maximum paid. However, even those authors who get little or nothing from the scheme are agreed that the principle is laudable, and they can always hope that at some future date the payment per loan will be substantially increased, which might make some reward possible for those whose books, although essential reading within their field, have a strictly limited readership. (Unfortunately, since British Governments, of whatever political persuasion, are notoriously niggardly towards the Arts, and especially so where Literature is concerned, a large increase is likely to remain a pipe dream.)

An additional benefit of PLR is that, when your statement arrives in February of each year, you see the estimate of how many times your book (or each of your books if more than one has been published) has been borrowed during the year ended the previous June 30th. You cannot tell for how long it was borrowed, so it could be that it was taken out one day and brought back, unread, the next but at least all those people were interested enough to borrow it, and probably a large number of them actually read it from cover to cover. That can be very encouraging, especially for an author whose books do not chalk up enormous sales.

In order to qualify for PLR, you must be resident in the UK and have had a book published which is available in this country; obviously, if your book is not in the Public Libraries there will be no borrowings from which you might benefit. It is essential that the book has an ISBN (International Standard Book Number) since borrowings are recorded by reading the ISBNs into a computer. (Each book has its own ISBN, from which it may be identified throughout the world. Publishers normally allocate an ISBN to each of the books which they publish; for self-published books see page 122.) It is for the author to register a book or books for PLR. Apply in the first place to The Registrar, Public Lending Right Office; you will be sent a form to fill in and return. There is no registration fee, and it will cost you no more than the two second-class stamps you will use. The list of registered books closes on June 30th in each year, so prior to that date you should inform the PLR office of any new titles which should go on the list of your books which are eligible for payment.

The payment of PLR moneys takes place in February each year, covering the twelve months ending on June 30th of the previous year. Payments can be made direct to your bank or building society.

At present, PLR payments continue for 70 years after the author's death, but there is a possibility that this period will be reduced at some future date in order to release more money for living authors. It is not likely to go down to less than 20 years after death.

The UK was among the first countries to set up the PLR scheme in the early 1980s, but was preceded by both Sweden and Denmark. Since then, other European countries have instituted similar schemes. Indeed an EU directive demands that all member countries should draw up and pass the relevant legislation to bring their own PLR into being. Outside Europe, several other PLR arrangements exist, including those in Australia, New Zealand and Canada. At the moment, most schemes are restricted to nationals of the countries concerned, but the UK has an arrangement with Germany whereby we pay PLR fees to German authors on borrowings of their books from our libraries, and they pay British authors similarly, and it is hoped that this reciprocity will spread to other countries. It would also be good news if the USA, which seems to lag behind in such matters, were to come into line.

Authors' Licensing and Collecting Society

The Authors' Licensing and Collecting Society (ALCS) was set up in 1977 in order to collect and distribute to its members certain moneys which they are unable to receive directly themselves. For instance, German PLR fees due to British authors cannot by German law be paid directly to those authors but must be sent in bulk, as it were, to an agency which will undertake its distribution, and the ALCS fills that role. Other similar payments come from PLR schemes in other countries, and from such uses as private and off-air recording, licensed educational recording, certain electronic rights, simultaneous cable television transmissions (the simultaneous showing of television signals in foreign countries via a cable network) and some public performances. But the biggest source of income so far has resulted from the work of the Copyright Licensing Agency (see below), which has been mainly concerned with reprography (the photocopying of printed material).

Large sums of money are involved, and the sums due are normally paid in February, May, August and November. In the year 1998–99, the ALCS distributed to its 35,000 members no less than £9.4 million. The moneys are paid directly to the authors, rather than to publishers or agents, after the deduction of a small commission in order to finance the operation. However, it is possible to arrange for payments to be made to agents, and it will not surprise authors to learn that agents are increasingly of the opinion that they are entitled to take their normal percentage of the ALCS moneys, especially those derived from television rights.

The total amount paid out by the ALCS rises each year, and can be expected to continue to increase as the Copyright Licensing Agency expands its control of the photocopying of copyright material, and as more foreign countries adopt PLR and use the ALCS to distribute the moneys.

The ALCS has also recently undertaken the distribution of moneys which it has mandated the Copyright Licensing Agency to collect in respect of Digitisation (the copying of printed material by the use of a scanner, the image then being stored within a computer, and viewed only on a computer screen – see below). It seems likely that the licensing fees for this new form of reproduction of written material will prove as lucrative as those for reprography.

As I write, the ALCS is negotiating with the Newspaper Licensing Agency for an agreement to pass on to freelance journalists the income from the photocopying of their work in newspapers.

The ALCS is administered by its Chief Executive and office staff, but is controlled by a Board, one third of the members of which are appointed by the Society of Authors, one third by the Writers' Guild of Great Britain, and one third directly elected by the membership as whole.

Membership of the ALCS is free and automatic to all members of the Society of Authors and the Writers' Guild, and limited free membership is available to members of the National Union of Journalists, the Chartered Institute of Journalists, the British Association of Journalists and the British Comedy Writers'

Association. For those who do not come under any of those headings, the annual subscription for UK residents is £5.88 (inclusive of VAT) – or £5 for residents in EU countries, or £7 for other foreign residents. Some moneys received by the ALCS from foreign sources are not allocated by those sources to individual authors, so the Society sends an equal share of these sums to each of its members; since the amount you get is well in excess of the annual subscription, it is obviously worth joining, even if you do not expect to earn anything from other sources. To apply for membership, write to: Membership Administrator, The Authors' Licensing and Collecting Society. It is important when joining to send a full list of your published work, together with the ISBNs, where appropriate, and this should be updated when you publish or broadcast any new works.

Copyright Licensing Agency

The development of reprography (photocopying) in the 1970s led to the establishment in 1982 of the Copyright Licensing Agency (CLA). The organisation is run by a Chief Executive and his staff, reporting to a Board consisting of representatives of authors, in the shape of the Chief Executive and nominated Committee Members of the ALCS, and nominees of the Publishers Licensing Society (PLS), which in turn represents the Publishers Assoc-iation, the Periodical Publishers Association and the Association of Learned and Professional Society Publishers.

When the CLA first began to operate, it was clear that photo-copying was in many cases a gross infringement of copyright: large companies would make scores of photocopies of an article in a magazine so that all members of their staff who needed to see it would have a copy; schools, lacking the money to buy a textbook in sufficient numbers would simply photocopy pages from it, or even the whole book; amateur drama societies would buy one copy of a play and then photocopy it; and so on. With the force of the existing copyright laws, bolstered later by the Copyright, Designs and Patents Act 1988, the CLA set about informing such infringers that what they were doing was illegal, and persuading them firstly to buy additional copies of the book or journal or, if that should be impractical, then to take out a licence allowing photocopies to be made. The CLA was careful to pitch its fees at a level which seemed, at least in most cases, reasonable to the user. This, together with the serious threat of legal action against offenders, resulted in the signing of many licensing agreements. It was not possible, of course, to catch the individual who would go to the library or copyshop to make copies of a play or whatever it might be. The CLA has, however, made it clear to those in charge of what might be called public photocopiers that, while there is no restriction on the making of a single photocopy, for personal use only, of a short extract from a book or of a single article from a magazine, anything more than that is illegal.

The very substantial sums accruing from the licences which the CLA grants are usually split, in the case of books, 50/50 between the authors, represented by the ALCS, and the publishers, represented by the PLS, while moneys resulting from the photocopying of articles, which used to go exclusively to the PLS, are now split so that a 25% share of the proceeds is paid to the ALCS for onward transmission to authors. Some variations on these figures may occur in respect of course packs for educational use.

Individual authors who are members of the ALCS do not need to take any action in order to benefit from the CLA's activities, since it is the ALCS and the publishers jointly who give the CLA a mandate to issue licences for the photocopying of their work in books, journals or magazines. It is hoped that the licensing scheme will soon be expanded to cover the work of freelance journalists published in newspapers.

The CLA is also currently widening its activities in order to control the electronic use of copyright material. This work will clearly prove of great value as the Internet becomes an even more important method of communication than it is now. At present the CLA is concentrating on digitisation (the reproduction and storage of printed material in a computer). As with reprography, the CLA will be issuing digitisation licences to colleges of further and higher education, universities, pharmaceutical and other companies – in short, to very much the same outlets as are presently licensed in respect of reprography.

As technology develops, the CLA will undoubtedly keep abreast of the changes. There may indeed be other electronic forms of reproduction, the monitoring of which will be undertaken under mandates from the ALCS. However, the situation is an extremely complex one, and the Association of Authors' Agents is seriously concerned that such mandates may in some cases be an infringement of rights already granted elsewhere. It is very important therefore to take advice on this subject from your agent, if you have one, or from the Society of Authors or the Writers' Guild.

The author as a marketable commodity

Once you have published a book or a considerable body of work in some other medium, or have had a play professionally performed, even if your success is comparatively modest, you are quite likely to have become marketable as an expert or a performer.

As an expert in the particular subject of your published work you might be asked to appear on radio or television, or to give lectures, and so on. In many cases a fee will be payable (this does not apply to appearances on local radio to promote your latest book – the companies feel that they are giving you quite enough in the form of publicity.) But the biggest opportunities probably lie in the field of teaching, or trying to teach, other people to write.

If you have any inclination in that direction, you can consider becoming a tutor of Creative Writing (so called mainly to distinguish it from calligraphy) for your local Adult Education Authority or for the WEA (Workers' Educational Association). The work itself is pleasant, but quite demanding, especially since the tutor is usually expected not merely to lecture on writing, but to read students' work and provide written comments on it, which cannot be done during class time. The classes usually follow the same pattern as in schools: three terms in the year, but only once a week. Tutors are usually engaged if sufficient students enrol for the term in question. The fees which the author-tutor receives are likely to be about £28 per two-hour class, but there is no additional payment for the substantial amount of work that you will have to do in your own time, and no allowance for travel and other expenses. The local education authority will also probably insist that you undergo some training as a tutor.

You can also contact the Regional Arts Association for your area and get yourself put on their list of writers prepared to give talks in schools. The fees for such engagements are usually subsidised by the RAA, and are therefore reasonably generous.

Creative Writing courses are offered at many universities nowadays; if you became a tutor you would not only have a secure living wage, but also free time in which to get on with your own writing. The snag is that, to be accepted, you would need good academic qualifications and a high literary reputation. In rather more down-to-earth vein, you might be asked to give a one-off lecture to the students – some tutors like to bring in someone from the coalface to tell the students what it's really like out there in the hard commercial world. The payment received for giving such a lecture is not enormous, but worth the effort involved.

You should be aware that if you are employed by universities or local education authorities Income Tax and National Health contributions are likely to be deducted from your fees.

In addition to classes and lectures, some educational author-ities, writers' conferences and literary festivals ask authors to conduct workshops. The Arts Council of England recommends a minimum fee of £150 for a workshop but, if the organisation putting on the event is a small one, the fee offered may be nowhere near that level. You will have to decide not only whether this is work for which you are suited but what your own minimum fee will be.

You may also find yourself in demand as a judge of literary competitions. As with the major Festivals, you have to be very successful and pretty famous to be asked to be a judge for the Booker or the Whitbread or the other important prizes, but lesser-known authors are often asked to select the winners for less well-publicised competitions, including those for short stories or poetry. The fees are usually fairly modest but, in some cases, an extra sum is payable if you are expected to provide detailed comments on any or all of the entries.

Magazines for writers provide an outlet for instructional articles on various aspects of writing. If you can supply punchy material, especially if it covers old problems with a new angle and in a practical way, you might find yourself with a regular column.

Yet another possibility is that you will be approached by would-be authors with a request that you should read their books (usually fiction) and give them professional advice on them. This, as with teaching Creative Writing and judging competitions, is not something on which you should embark unless you feel capable of putting your finger on the faults and offering constructive criti-cism. The fees tend to vary according to the financial situation of the author concerned and the length of the book, but would normally be a minimum of £50, rising to perhaps £200.

As less of a teacher and rather more of a performer, assuming that you have the time available, you can build a useful addition to your income by giving talks to writers' circles, Women's Institutes, Townswomen's Guilds, Probus Clubs and the like. There are three requirements: the first is something of general interest to say, with your material fashioned so that it has a shape to it – a beginning, a middle and an end – and preferably a few jokes here and there, which provide variety and help to keep your audience awake; the second is a willingness to be the centre of attention – this is no job for shrinking violets; and the third is the ability to pitch your voice so that you are audible at the back of the room or hall where you are speaking.

As for the financial rewards, the Arts Council of England recommends that you should receive a minimum fee of £100 for a talk, but this is quite unrealistic at the level of local societies and groups. The fees offered are in fact modest, but once you have assembled the material for a talk you can use it again and again, so that comparatively little work is involved, and for that reason you may feel that the reward is in fact a little more worthwhile than it sounds.

Writers' circles (which may prefer an instructive talk rather than one which is merely entertaining), especially those with no more than a handful of members, can often barely afford to pay expenses, let alone a sizeable fee, but many authors feel that the temptation to make no charge should be resisted – the professional (which is what you are) is worthy of some sort of hire, even if it is little more than a token, and if you give your services free you will be letting down your fellow authors as a whole. On the other hand, there are those who believe that you should be generous and either not take a fee at all unless the group to which you speak is clearly wealthy, or should give the fee to a charity, such as the Authors' Foundation.

Much more rewarding are appearances as a speaker at one of the many conferences for writers, such as the week-long Writers' Summer School at Swanwick in August and Writers' Holiday at Caerleon, South Wales, in July, and the shorter Scottish Association of Writers' Weekend Conference in April, and the Writers' Conference at Winchester in June, etc. The talks which are wanted by such organisations are required to be basically about writing (general advice, especially about techniques and markets), but should also be entertaining. Main speakers at such events are likely to receive £100 to £200, and the same applies to minor Literary Festivals (the speakers at major Festivals, such as that held at Edinburgh, are likely to be big-name authors who expect and get big-name fees).

Women's Institutes and Townswomen's Guilds tend to pay between £15 and £30 for a forty minute talk, plus travelling expenses. Probus Clubs may be a little more generous and will also usually provide a lunch or dinner, but Rotary Clubs, which are always concerned to give as much money as possible to charity, are likely to give you only the food. None of these organisations will expect to make any deductions for Income Tax and will not normally pay VAT, except in the form of an all-inclusive fee (see pages 93–4).

Incidentally, to get on to the Women's Institutes circuit you will need to apply to your WI County Federation, asking to be put on the list for their next Speakers' Day. The Speakers' Days are in fact auditions, attended by representatives of the WIs in the county. Once you pass muster at the Speakers' Day, you are put on the Federation's list of approved speakers, engagements will then follow and, if you are successful, word-of-mouth recommendations will ensure that you find yourself regularly in demand. You should be aware, of course, that if you are available to give talks only in the evening, you will be cutting yourself off from the large number of Institutes which meet in the afternoon or morning. The problem is less acute with Townswomen's Guilds, while the majority of Probus Clubs gather at lunchtime.

None of this will happen unless you do something about it. If you go to your local library you will be able to find out where you should apply to become a tutor of Creative Writing, or a Women's Institute or Townswomen's Guild speaker. Join your local Writers' Circle (they will be delighted to welcome a published author). Let it be known in your neighbourhood that you are an author – people are bound to be interested because writers have a certain glamour about them, even if you and I know that we're just as ordinary as everyone else – and do everything you can to promote yourself. You may be very shy, but public speaking is not as difficult as it may seem. You will probably enjoy it, once you get going, as long as you speak clearly and loudly and have prepared what you are going to say in advance (you could even write it all out, but try not to read it, or if you must do so, at least try to look as though you're not reading).

A different form of entertainment which has become popular in recent years is provided by an author reading from his or her work, especially in the form of Performance Poetry. The Arts Council of England recommends a minimum fee of £100 for a reading (and says that £150 would be more reasonable), but again authors are likely to receive only what those who are running the event can afford. Many small organisations are non-profit-making, and the fees will be based on the expected income from the audience.

All these activities have an important benefit beyond the extra money that they may bring in. You will be promoting your work as well as yourself, and in many cases you will have an opportunity of selling copies of your book or books (see below). For example, when performance poetry takes place in pubs, it is unlikely that the poets taking part will receive any fees; they will, however, have an audience to listen to their work and can often sell useful quantities of the printed versions of their poems. You can find out from local papers and libraries and, for the more formal occasions, from the Regional Arts Boards, where performance poetry is taking place.

If, like many authors, you are very disappointed by what your publisher does in the way of publicity (don't forget, however, that some of the firm's activities in this direction may not be immediately visible to you), remember that it is possible, in the ways outlined above, to promote yourself and to get paid for doing so. It is important, however, to be aware that you will be liable to pay Income Tax on any such earnings.

Payment of expenses

Almost all organisations which hire authors as speakers or tutors are prepared to pay travelling expenses, but do not normally expect to foot the bill for first-class train fares or indeed any other form of 'luxury' transport. In many cases, the treasurer or the accounts department, or whoever is paying the money, will want to see evidence of the charge you are making, and groups such as the Women's Institutes will pay public transport fares, and usually have a set mileage fee for those travelling in their own cars (the WIs currently allow 22p per mile). You will also get a cup of tea, accompanied by anything from one biscuit to a feast. If you are invited to a writers' conference or a festival, board and lodging will almost certainly be provided for you, but it is worth discovering in advance just what extras, such as wines and other drinks, will be included.

If your publishers ask you to go on a publicity tour, you can expect that all your expenses will be paid. And if you travel, for instance, to make a local broadcast, your publishers may be willing to refund you the costs which you have paid.

As for the expenses involved in research, these are normally the author's responsibility and you are likely to be paid for them only if it has been so agreed in the contract, which is likely only in exceptional cases.

Prizes, grants and bursaries

In the years immediately before the Second World War and for a considerable period thereafter, critics wielded considerable power and it was they who could turn a book or a play into an overnight success by reviewing it in terms of unstinted praise. Critics rarely have so much influence nowadays and it may be argued that their place as promoters of exciting new work has been taken by the groups who award prizes. Prizes are not merely flavour of the month, they have been so for some decades and look likely to continue to give their winners a tremendous sales boost. Even those which are awarded for work in a highly specialised field, although they rarely get mentioned in the national press, can bring the author fame and fortune among those who are passionate about the subject.

There are probably few fields in which so many prizes are awarded as that of literary work. In the edition of the *Writers' and Artists' Yearbook* which is current as I write, no fewer than 31 pages are devoted to prizes and awards and, although some of them are for artists or photographers, the majority are for the written word, including works for radio, television and the stage, and journalism. The actual prizes range from little more than the honour of winning, plus perhaps a medal, to what is at present the most valuable prize of all, the International IMPAC Dublin Literary Award of IR£100,000 for a work of fiction written in English. The most prestigious prize of all is the Nobel in Literature but for that, of course, an author needs an international reputation and to have produced a considerable body of work of a high literary standard.

In Britain the most coveted prizes remain the Booker, the Whitbread Prizes and the Orange. The Booker and the Orange are exclusively for novels, while the Whitbread has prizes for a novel, a biography/autobiography, a children's book and a first novel. Among the other prizes more are for fiction than for any other genre, but there are awards for poetry, biography, history, short stories, essays, children's books, sport and many other varieties of specialist non-fiction, and, as already mentioned, for drama, radio and television material and journalism. Some prizes are specifically for the author's first published work and others make reference to the author's age. In most cases the work concerned has to have been published but some are restricted to unpublished material.

It is usual for work entered for any of the prizes to be submitted by the publishers but that, of course, does not apply to unpublished work. Details of where to apply for further information are given in the *Writers' and Artists' Yearbook*.

In addition to the prizes, a number of grants, bursaries and fellowships are available, most of which are intended to help writers to complete a given piece of work, either by financing the necessary research or, in some more generous cases, by providing the author with a supplement to any existing receipts, thus raising the income to a level on which it may be more possible to exist. The main source of such grants is the Arts Council of England and its Regional Arts Boards, the Arts Council of Wales, the Scottish Arts Council and the Arts Council of Ireland, but there are several other foundations and associations which assist authors in this way, including a number administered by the Society of Authors. Details of where to apply for such grants are given in the *Writers' and Artists' Yearbook*.

Finally, mention should be made of the Royal Literary Fund. It is not concerned with subsidising research or a particular writing project, but with supplying financial support for professional authors and their families who have fallen on hard times. The Francis Head Bequest works in a similar way, under the aegis of the Society of Authors.

Prizes are not generally taxable, unless the work was written specifically for a prize, as in a competition. Grants and bursaries tend to be taxable when they are given in order to meet specific professional expenses, usually in connection with a particular writing project.

Competitions

Literary competitions, mostly for poetry or short stories, abound. Of course, they could well be included under the 'Prizes' heading above, but they are usually for unpublished work and, being smaller in scope, do not attract interest in the national press. Indeed, some competitions are quite minor, perhaps based on a local theme and limited to people living in the neighbourhood, while others, such as the Bridport Prize or the Poetry Society's National Poetry Competition have considerable prestige as well as substantial cheques for the winners. Most competitions charge between £2 and £5 an entry (that's where the prize money and the adjudicator's fee come from) and entering them regularly can be quite expensive. However, many writers do submit their work despite the fee, because to be among the prize-winners, or even to be told that their work has been shortlisted, is enormously encouraging, quite apart from any financial reward.

The conditions for entry vary from competition to competition. Most, as already mentioned, insist that anything submitted should not have been published previously. Some impose a further condition by saying that work should not have been entered for any other competition (though how they can tell if you break that rule, I am not sure). There is almost always a restriction on the length of entries. In some cases the competition will require that the story or poem should be on a set subject. Unless it is made clear that only previously unpublished writers may enter, there is nothing to stop well-established writers from submitting their work (a number usually do and it is interesting to note that they are not always among the winners).

One entry rule to beware of is the organisation's right to publish the winning entries, perhaps in a booklet of their own or in a local newspaper. That is fine, and may indeed add to the prestige of winning, but it is important to check that there is no question of the author surrendering copyright.

Competitions are advertised in magazines for writers (*Writers News* itself regularly runs a great many competitions) and often in local newspapers. Every writers' circle in the country receives details and entry forms for a large number of competitions.

Selling copies of your books

Most publishers' contracts contain a clause saying that the author is entitled to buy copies of his or her book at a stated discount, or perhaps at 'best trade terms' (it is preferable to have a discount specified, rather than 'best trade terms' which the publishers are free to define in a number of possibly ungenerous ways). Many publishers supply their authors at a 35 per cent discount, but some do better than that and some worse – there is no consistency in the matter.

The clause allowing you to buy books at trade terms then usually goes on to say that such copies are 'not for resale', a proviso which has appeared in contracts for donkey's years, intended to preserve the structure of the trade, the publisher's relationship with booksellers and, indeed, the booksellers' livelihoods. However, most publishers have come to accept that if authors have the chance of selling copies of their books, the chance should be taken and is, in any case, unlikely to harm sales through bookshops.

Incidentally, for many years the restriction that books bought by the author were not for resale was fairly strictly enforced, with the result that the author, in most cases, did not buy the books in large quantities. It was usual for them to ask that their cost be debited to the royalty account. Nowadays, publishers don't much like that system. Authors who sell quite large quantities of their books in this way – and many of them do – will owe the publishers a substantial sum; if the advance has not yet been earned or the royalties available are not big enough to cover the charges, the publishers will lose money on the deal.

The chance to sell books occurs when the author is making a public appearance of some sort – perhaps addressing a luncheon club or a Women's Institute or something similar, and especially if participating in a writers' conference or festival. Although it might be considered that authors have some sort of duty towards booksellers and should not deprive them of any sales, it is really a question of a bird in the hand – many of those who hear the author speak will buy copies of his/her books if they are there on the spot and the author is willing to sign them. For some conferences a local bookshop has a presence, and will have copies of the books by the speakers. Their sales are undoubtedly boosted by the presence of those speakers, but it is still possible for the authors to bypass them and sell direct, even if this does not greatly increase their popularity with the booksellers.

Another sales possibility exists if you are on the Internet, and can produce your own website in which you give information about your book, probably with a coloured illustration of the jacket, and solicit sales. You will need to enter the website into the various search engines under a variety of category headings which will attract to the site those who might be interested. You may not wish to put your private address on the website, but you can ask any potential customers to get in touch with you via e-mail.

Since you will be able to buy the books from the publishers at a discount and sell them at full list price, you will obviously make a profit. You are, of course, liable to pay tax on that profit. You should end up comfortably in the black, since you will also receive your normal royalty on the copies that you buy from the publishers. Don't, by the way, sell your books at less than the list price which the publishers have placed on them. To give a discount really does undermine small booksellers and the publishers' sales force and makes it awkward for other writers who are selling their books at the full price.

The profit on selling your own books can become substantial if your publishers decide to remainder one or more of your titles. Of course, it is a sad day when the publishers decide that the sales of a book are non-existent, or so slow that it is not worth keeping the book in stock. It happens, unfortunately to a great many books, despite the publishers' best efforts, and not only to the notoriously difficult-to-establish first novels by unknown authors. Remaindered books are to be seen mostly in bookshops dedicated to selling bargain books at really knock-down prices. Most contracts contain a clause obliging the publisher to offer the author the opportunity of buying copies of the books at the remainder price (that is, the price which a 'remainder merchant' has offered to pay in order to take the unsold stock off the publishers' hands). If you can afford to buy a substantial quantity (and have the room to store them – books in bulk need a lot of space), you may well over a few years dispose of them at the full published price. You can sell them when the publisher can't, because you and the books are there at a writers' conference, perhaps, and you are willing to sign them, and you have just given a wonderful talk, and large numbers of your audience are queuing up to buy.

7. Income Tax, VAT and Self-Employment

Income Tax

Regularly every year that dreaded brown envelope arrives enclosing a form on which your income has to be entered so that Her Majesty's Tax Inspectors may decide how much tax you have to pay. Any money that you earn from writing, whether it comes as an advance, or as royalties, or as the payment of expenses, is taxable. If you don't know already, it will not surprise you to learn that, as with all tax matters, the rules governing tax on an author's earnings are complicated.

The first thing that has to be established with the Inland Revenue is that you are a professional author, which does not necessarily mean that writing is your only occupation, but that you are writing regularly with the intention of selling your work. If the income that you earn from your pen is spasmodic and small in quantity, the Inland Revenue will regard your writing as a sideline, and will not accord you the benefits available to a professional. Unless your writing income is really no more than peanuts, a good accountant will be able to argue effectively your case for being regarded as a professional. Mind you, if you need an accountant for this particular reason, it will probably cost you more than you save. If you do not have an accountant, or can't afford one, it will be worth seeking the advice of the Society of Authors or the Writers' Guild or the National Union of Journalists or the Institute of Journalists, or any similar body to which you belong in order to learn the best way of approaching the problem.

At the time of writing, a professional author is usually taxed under Schedule D, Case II, of the 1988 Income and Corporation Taxes Act, while the author whose work is classified by the Inland Revenue as a sideline will be taxed under the less beneficial Schedule D, Case VI. Schedule D is that part of the Act which sets out the rules for the taxation of the self-employed. Naturally, if you are employed as a writer on a full-time basis, as is the case with many journalists, tax on your salary will be deducted at source, under the P.A.Y.E. system, but if you write in your spare time and sell the work, that part of your income will come under Schedule D.

A major change was introduced in 1999 under which authors are deemed to have received money in the tax year in which it was due to be paid, even if it did not reach them until some later date. Equally, any legitimate expenses due in a given tax year can be taken as having been paid in that year, even if in fact payment was delayed into the following year.

While most receipts from writing as a freelance are taxable, whether they are paid directly to you or to an agent, there are a few exceptions. Unless those in charge change their minds, the Inland Revenue will accept literary prizes and certain grants made by the Arts Council as tax free, but you or your accountant should check.

All expenses genuinely incurred as a professional author are deductible, and these include:

- agent's and accountant's fees
- stationery
- secretarial work
- postage, telephone and faxes (a proportion of the rental, if you use your domestic phone, as well as the cost of those calls made on business as an author)
- subscriptions to relevant societies
- the expenses of research
- petrol and car maintenance
- entertainment, travel and hotel expenses.

It is also possible to claim for the exclusive use for your writing of a room in your house, and for the cost of its heating and lighting and other domestic expenses, but there are some dangers attached to a claim based on full use, because that could make you liable for Capital Gains tax if you should move house. It is usually better to claim only partial use of the room and a suitable proportion of the expenses.

On the other hand, there is no problem in securing allowances for depreciation on capital equipment, such as typewriters, computers, office furniture and even cars.

All expenses claimed will normally be allowed, provided that each of them is fully justified in connection with your work as an author, including any activities, such as lecturing, tutoring, or assessing other people's work, which arise from it. However, in many cases the Inland Revenue may not be willing, on the grounds of 'dual use', to allow the entire claim. An obvious example of dual use might be the cost of travel and accommodation if you combine a visit to some location for research purposes with a holiday. Matters of this sort sometimes fall into a somewhat grey area. The attitude of the Tax Inspector may well be less punitive if it is clear that, in all sections of your return, you are being honest and not trying to cheat the system.

For the vast majority of writers their work is poorly rewarded (a recent Society of Authors survey revealed that 52% of those responding earned less than £10,000 per annum from writing, and it was clear that for at least three-quarters of that 52%, the actual figure earned was well under £5000). Since that is so, it is quite likely that your legitimate expenses will exceed your writing income, and in that case you may be able to set off your loss for tax purposes against any other taxable income which you may have. Again, however, you must be able to show that you are a professional author who works regularly and does receive payment for your work, and not simply a hopeful but unsuccessful amateur for whom writing is no more than a sideline. Of course, you cannot claim any tax allowances for expenses in connection with your writing unless you have earned taxable income against which the allowances can be set.

The British Government, whether Tory or New Labour, is pretty philistine in its attitude towards the Arts, unlike, for instance, Eire, where authors do not pay any tax on their income from writing. However, the Inland Revenue in Britain at least understands that the money which flows or dribbles into an author's bank account does so unpredictably, possibly varying from a large sum in this or that year to practically nothing in the next. To meet this problem, concessions are available to enable you, in certain circumstances, to spread the moneys received over two or three years after first publication or performance of the work in order to pay at a less punitive rate of tax. Clearly, this will only be of use if the sums involved are reasonably large. Some relief is also available, again depending on the circumstances, if you resell your work ten or more years after its original publication or performance, but not if, at the time when the work first appeared, you spread the moneys received in respect of that work.

It should be made clear that selling your work for an outright sum, whether or not the copyright was included in the deal, does not mean that the moneys received are tax free. They have to be declared on your tax return just like any other income. On the other hand, most awards and prizes for literary work are not taxable, being really in the same class as a win on the National Lottery. Some Tax Inspectors have been difficult on this question in the past, have continued to demand payment of tax and, in a few cases, may have been correct in so doing – for instance, when the work has been written primarily with the intention of meeting the criteria demanded by the organisers of the award or prize. Advice on the subject is available from the professional bodies for writers.

An interesting point arises in respect of fees paid for lectures and talks given to Writers' Circles and Conferences, Women's Institutes, Townswomen's Guilds, Probus and Rotary Clubs, Literary Festivals, and the like, and for appearances on radio or television. Most organisations will pay the relevant fee without deduction of tax, leaving it to the recipient to declare the earnings to the Inland Revenue and pay the relevant tax in due course. Difficulties have arisen in the past with certain authorities and universities, who apparently wanted, because of a rigid pay structure, to class visiting lecturers as employees, which meant the deduction from their fees not only of Income Tax but of National Insurance payments as well. If you have met this problem in the past, but not recently, you may think that it is still possible to circumvent it by making sure that the letter of engagement states firmly that the author is giving a one-off lecture, rather than a course, for a fee, rather than a salary. However, it now seems that, at least with certain such authorities, the tax officials who are concerned with the authorities' accounts are insisting that tax and National Insurance should be deducted in all cases, even if you are paying National Insurance through your main job, which is not writing. If you have passed the age when National Insurance is payable, you can avoid that deduction by presenting the authority with proof of your age, but nothing will stop them taking off the tax. Of course, you can show that you have paid the amount they have deducted when making your annual return.

For work sold abroad, you would be liable to pay tax in any country in which you earned money as well as in the United Kingdom, were it not for the fact that the UK has Double Taxation Agreements with nearly all the developed countries of the world. You will have to fill in the necessary forms, which are available from the foreign purchaser or from your Tax Office, and have them certified. You will still have to include the sums in your UK tax return and pay UK tax on them, but you won't have to pay tax in the country from which the money came. This also applies if the work is sold abroad by an agent, except that it will be easier because you will have the agent's guidance. In the case of the rights being sold by publishers or a management of some kind, you should not have a problem, because the publishers or management will have made the deal as a principal and collected the money under the firm's own tax exemption arrangements. If you live abroad, you will, of course, be subject to the tax laws in your country of residence.

Employing an accountant

As may be gathered from all that has already been said in this chapter (and this material is inevitably little more than a summary of the main points which may affect the taxation of an author's income), the complexities of Income Tax as far as authors are concerned are such that it is likely to be extremely difficult for anyone but an expert to deal with the question satisfactorily. It does not help that not all Tax Inspectors are familiar with the various ways that authors are paid, and may not even be aware of all the legitimate claims that can be made. Unless your income from writing is minuscule and your expenses are minimal, or you are yourself expert in the matter, it is advisable to seek assistance.

You may think that if you have an agent, he or she will be competent to help you in this matter, but although agents usually have a working knowledge of what an author may be able to do in respect of tax allowances, they are not experts in that particular field and, in any case, do not have the time to give anything more than rough general guidance. Publishers and other purchasers of your work are likely to be of little if any assistance. Professional organisations, such as the Society of Authors and the Writers' Guild, can offer useful help and may have specific advice for certain circumstances, such as the tax situation with regard to prizes and awards, but they cannot be expected to provide a detailed service in this respect. You need to go to an accountant or at least a tax consultant. Although this will probably cost you upwards of £300 per annum, depending on the amount of work to be done, the fees are tax-deductible. In any case, by ensuring that all your legitimate claims are made, you will almost certainly save quite a bit of tax.

Of course, the figures which the accountant or tax consultant prepares and the return which is subsequently submitted to the Inland Revenue are based on the information you supply. Any accountant will ask you to keep the strictest possible records and this is just as necessary if you deal with the Tax Inspector yourself. Keep all receipts, copies of any invoices that you issue, details of payments received and full notes on your expenditure, so that you can say exactly what you spent and when and why. Have a notebook by your telephone, and make a record of all your business calls. Keep a post book for letters and parcels.

An idea which may help is to open a bank account which you use exclusively for your writing moneys; some bank managers may insist on making a charge on the grounds that the account is a business one. Unless it is a busy account, dealing with large sums of money and many entries and withdrawals, you could shop around until you find a bank or building society which will not charge. If you keep a ledger in which you record all your expenditure under various headings it will be easy at your year-end to tot up the figures to see what you have spent on telephone charges, subscriptions, travel, reference books, or whatever it may be.

Another possibility is to keep a credit card which you use exclusively for expenditure in connection with your writing. Again this will make the preparation of year-end accounts much simpler. You might do worse than to apply for the HSBC's Arts Card, which allows its users to select from a number of arts charities which of them will receive a small percentage of the moneys you spend using the card – the appropriate charity in this case is the Authors' Foundation.

Some authors, especially those who claim with not a little pride to be totally innumerate, prefer to dump all their papers on their accountants or tax consultants and let them sort it all out. That's fine, if you want to work that way, but you will almost certainly be charged much more than if you present everything in a more orderly fashion.

See also pages 108–9.

Value Added Tax

You do not need to worry about registering for Value Added Tax (VAT) unless you earn £50,000 a year or more as a self-employed person, in which case you have to register whether you like it or not. If you happen to earn more than that magic sum in a single year because of a major sale of rights, you may be able to avoid registration if you can persuade the VAT authorities that the earning is exceptional, and that in subsequent years you will revert to your more usual substantially lower income.

If you regularly earn less than £50,000 a year you are entitled to apply for voluntary registration for VAT, but this is hardly worth while unless you are paying a great deal of VAT on essential expenses, agent's fees, accountant's fees, capital equipment and the like. The reason why it is not recommended is primarily the amount of time a VAT-registered author has to spend on keeping records of all VAT which he or she pays, ensuring that all moneys received include VAT, making quarterly returns to HM Customs and Excise, which organisation may wish to visit the author and examine the accounts in lengthy and painstaking detail. The returns have to be made by the author, rather than by an agent or accountant, although you will undoubtedly find it helpful (and perhaps even essential) to employ your accountant to maintain your VAT records and prepare your returns.

An additional reason for not becoming VAT-registered is that small organisations, such as Women's Institutes or Writers' Circles, do not normally expect to pay VAT on your fee. This means that if you are registered, you must insist on getting the agreed fee plus 17½%. If you accept the agreed fee as being inclusive of VAT, it means that your actual earnings amount to approximately 85.1% of what you receive.

Once you have registered for VAT, which you do by contacting your local VAT Office, you are given a VAT Registration Number which you must quote not only on all your correspondence regarding VAT, but on any invoices which you may issue for work of various kinds, including lecturing and public appearances as well as written material. You must also inform publishers and managers, and any other sources of your income. They will then pay advances and royalties and subsidiary rights income plus VAT on the services that you have provided (i.e. in selling them a licence to publish your work, which puts you in the position similar to that of a freelance employee).

You also collect vouchers for any expenditure directly related to your work, and then offset the VAT paid out against the VAT received, and either pay or claim back the balance from the VAT authorities. An agent (who is in effect your employee) will charge you VAT on the agency's percentage of moneys handled on your behalf whether or not you are registered for VAT. So will an accountant, so will the petrol station where you fill up your car, and so will most goods and services which you use in your capacity of an author. However, while the standard VAT rate is 17½%, domestic fuel and power are rated at 8%, and books and newspapers and magazines, and coach, rail and air travel, are all zero-rated. You are not expected to pay VAT for services from people who are not themselves registered, or on subscriptions to professional bodies, such as the Society of Authors and the Writers' Guild, or on wages, insurance, rates, rent of private properties, or on taxi fares. Of course it is important to take note of any changes to VAT which the Chancellor of the Exchequer may announce from time to time.

If you are not registered for VAT you must not invoice anyone for VAT, and naturally you cannot claim for the VAT which you pay out.

Is it all too complicated? That's why registration is best avoided. However, if you feel that you should be registered, the Society of Authors, the Writers' Guild and similar organisations, while they cannot act as accountants, are able, as with Income Tax, to give advice to their members on basic problems relating to VAT.

Self-employment

If you earn money from freelance writing, you are deemed by officialdom to be self-employed, provided that the writing is not done as a part or the whole of your employment by another person or company, as, for instance, in the case of a journalist on the staff of a newspaper. If you are commissioned to write something, that does not mean that whoever commissions you is your employer – a contract to write a book or a play or whatever it may be is not a contract of employment. You are still, in effect, an independent freelance.

It is also possible to be both employed and self-employed, when your employer does not in any way control the work that you do as a self-employed person. This is the position of many regularly published authors who hold down a job during the day and write in the evenings and at weekends.

However, if you decide to give up working for somebody else, and to devote yourself entirely to your writing, then you will be not only self-employed, but will be starting up a business. For most people, being your own boss is very pleasant – no more commuting, no more boredom or harassment in the office, and no need to ask anyone but yourself if you want to have an afternoon off or an extra week's holiday. However, self-employment does carry with it a number of obligations, not least that of being able, from your unpredictable earnings as a writer, to support yourself and any dependants that you may have. As the 1662 Book of Common Prayer says of marriage, it is not by any to be enterprised, nor taken in hand, unadvisedly, lightly, or wantonly.

If you are determined to become self-employed on a full-time basis, your first practical obligation will be to inform straight-away the Inland Revenue, the National Insurance Contributions office and your local Tax office of the change in your circumstances. You must also tell the Customs and Excise authorities about your business if you are likely to be liable for VAT (see above), and your Job Centre if you have previously been registered with one. You can get a booklet from your local Department of Social Security office which includes a form for you to fill in, and this single form will give the necessary information to the National Insurance, Inland Revenue and Customs and Excise authorities in one go. In all your dealings in these matters you will need to know your National Insurance number. If you have previously been in employment, you will have to send parts 2 and 3 of your P45 to the Inland Revenue with the form.

The Inland Revenue will require annual accounts from you, and you will need to decide on your year-end date, which can be the anniversary of starting the business, or December 31st, as the end of the calendar year, or April 5th, as the end of the tax year, or the end of any month.

The accounts will probably be acceptable in a simple form if your gross trading income is under £15,000, when you will merely need to state the gross figure, the expenses claimed, and the resultant net figure. If your turnover is greater than £15,000 you will be expected to provide formal accounts, consisting of a summary of the year's income and expenditure under various headings (such as 'fees received' on the credit side, and 'car expenses' or 'stationery' or 'postage and telephone' on the expenses side), plus a balance sheet, showing your assets (including equipment), moneys owing and debts not yet paid. You will probably need the help of an accountant if formal accounts are to be prepared.

It is certainly advisable to seek an accountant's advice when first setting up the business and deciding on your year-end date. The Inland Revenue has a nasty little arrangement whereby you may, during the first two years that you are in business, be taxed twice on some of your profits. It all depends on the length of time between your year-end date and the end of the tax year on April 5th, You can apparently be given a refund when your business ceases to exist, and since, for most authors, their business ceases only when they pop their clogs, it won't be much consolation for them to know that the refund will be part of their estate. However, a good accountant should be able to solve this problem for you.

If you are self-employed you must pay weekly National Insurance contributions if you are 16 or over but under retirement age (currently 60 for women, 65 for men), unless you have been exempted from liability. Contributions are normally paid by direct debit (monthly in arrears), or through a quarterly bill (also in arrears).

There are several classes of National Insurance contributions: Class 1 (or Class 1A if your employer provides you with a car for private use) is the normal payment if you work for an employer; for the self-employed Classes 2, 3 and 4 apply. Class 2 is the basic contribution, Class 3 is a voluntary contribution in lieu of and lower than the basic version, and Class 4 is at a higher rate, the extra being what might be regarded as a levy on those self-employed people who make a lot of money from their business.

You will be expected to pay under one of these three classes, unless you are exempted because your profits from your writings (i.e. your earnings less any expenses which the NI authorities will accept as justifiable deductions) are below a set level. However, if you apply for what is known as 'small earnings exception' and are excused from paying, your State Retirement Pension and other benefits may be affected. It will therefore be worth your while in the long run to pay the Class 2 contributions if you can possibly afford to do so. The alternative voluntary Class 3 contributions go some way towards protecting your benefits, but are not as satisfactory in this respect as keeping up the full Class 2 payments.

If your profits are above a certain level, you may have to pay Class 4 as well as Class 2 contributions, the former being paid along with your Income Tax, which sounds unfair, but which is based on the idea that the wealthy should pay more than those with small incomes. And if you are both employed and self-employed, you may find yourself paying three lots of contributions: Class 1 (via your employer), Class 2 because you are also self-employed, and Class 4 if your income rises above a specified level. However, you should be able to recoup some of the money if the total you pay is considered by the NI authorities to be excessive.

It is impossible to give any indication of the amounts involved in any of these contributions, since they are variable according to the Chancellor of the Exchequer's latest Budget. Equally, since the contributions you have to make are affected by so many different circumstances, the only sensible way of finding out how you stand is to go to your local Department of Social Security and go through your case with the people there.

It is perhaps worth pointing out that your NI contributions are not just a one-way traffic – they do provide benefits, such as child benefits, maternity pay, and other family benefits, statutory sick pay and pensions.

Pensions

Your NI contributions will in fact provide you with a State Pension when you reach retirement age. Of course, writers can go on writing and selling their work until the day they die (provided that they haven't lost their marbles). If you prefer to take things rather more easily or if, for any reason, you give up writing, you may feel that the State Pension is pretty inadequate. It will keep body and soul together, but that's about all. If you have been in some non-writing form of full employment for most of your life, with writing being no more than a sideline, you will no doubt receive an occupational pension. With any luck that will suffice to keep you more or less in the way to which you have become accustomed. Equally if you have been a bestselling author, you will probably have enough stashed away to see you out in your customary lifestyle without your having to worry about a pension. But if you have been a no-more-than-moderately successful full-time author, there will be nothing but the State Pension for you, unless you were prudent enough at as young an age as possible to take out some kind of pension scheme – and it may not be too late now . . .

'But,' you may say, 'Writing is a such a chancy business that I could never be certain of keeping up the necessary contributions.' In fact, most insurance companies operate schemes which allow you to pay annually a lump sum, the size of which depends on what you can afford at the time. Obviously, the more you can put in over a long period of years, the better the pension will be, but even if your contributions are small and erratic, at least they will guarantee you receipt of a sum to supplement what the State gives you. The plans offered by the different insurance firms differ slightly from company to company, so you should shop around.

The Society of Authors operates a non-contributory pension scheme, but it is available to a limited number of members only and is in the nature of a useful but comparatively small supplementary income. The Society advertises in its journal, *The Author*, when it has a vacancy for a member to join its roll of pensioners and asks for applications. The Royal Literary Fund also provides a limited number of pensions, on a slightly more generous scale, but with the proviso that the recipient must have published previously 'work of approved literary merit'. If you are of pensionable age, are in financial need and have the necessary qualifications as far as your published work is concerned, you can make application to the Fund.

The Writers' Guild has agreements with the Producers' Alliance of Cinema and Television, the BBC and other purchasers of its members' work which provide for pension contributions for the author to be made by both the purchaser and the author.

Becoming a Limited Company

There are advantages in making yourself a Limited Liability Company. Firstly, of course, it may offer you some protection if, for example, you are sued for some reason in connection with your writing – your liability to pay damages will be limited to the assets of the company and will not touch your personal moneys. However, it has to be said that in many cases the claimant may be able to pursue a case against you personally in your capacity as the author of the material which is the subject of the lawsuit.

The main benefit of becoming a Limited Company is that the tax on your earnings can be substantially lower, since Corporation Tax for small businesses currently runs at 20% on the first £32,335. It is also beneficial if you can afford to leave a substantial sum in the company, rather than withdrawing it. There is a further tax advantage in that, on the death of the author, the assets of the company are not treated as part of the taxable estate. However, there is little to be gained unless your earnings from writing are fairly substantial. Even then the Inland Revenue will probably argue that the earnings of a copyright-owning company should be treated as the personal income of the creator of the copyrights. There are also the disadvantages of having to prepare formal accounts, which will have to be properly audited (an extra expense), and, since you will be employed by your company, of having to pay National Insurance contributions at a higher rate.

The matter is a complex one, and you will need advice from your accountant. If it is decided that you should become a

Limited Liability company, your accountant will be able to prepare all the necessary paperwork, but if you should wish to go ahead on your own, you can obtain from Companies House (there are offices in Cardiff, London, Birmingham, Leeds, Manchester, Edinburgh and Glasgow) all the necessary forms, and a number of pamphlets giving advice on a variety of matters, including the preparation of the Memorandum and Articles of Association and Disclosure Requirements. You will need to say where the company's registered offices are, and the company will be required to have at least one director and another person as company secretary. You will also have to choose a company name, which is not as simple a matter as you might think, since you have to check with Companies House that no existing company is already using that name, or something too close in similarity to it. You may wish to avoid calling the Company by your own name, which most accountants seem to advise, in order principally to make it a little more difficult for members of the public at large to consult the company's records.

8. Sources of Help

Agents

It seems to be increasingly true that you cannot expect to get your work published or performed without the services of a literary agent, at least in the case of fiction – non-fiction and books for children, provided that the approach is original, may be easier to place without help. But the Catch-22 as far as new novelists, playwrights and some non-fiction writers are concerned, is that you have to have an agent to get started, but it is well nigh impossible to persuade any agent to take on a new client, or even to read a synopsis, unless that person already has a track record.

How do you overcome this Catch-22? The best advice is probably to submit work directly to publishers or to radio or television companies or to theatre managements, and to look for an agent only when an offer for the work has been made by publishers or other purchasers, and before the contract has been signed. It will be much easier to find an agent in those circumstances. You might think that a purchaser would object to an agent being brought in at this stage but, on the contrary, the company or management with which you are dealing may, without prompting, suggest a suitable agency – it is sometimes easier for them to deal with an agent whom they know, and who knows them, rather than with an author who is not conversant with trade practices.

If you still want to find an agent rather than submitting your work directly yourself to publishers or managements, then try the newer agencies – in most cases the firms listed in the *Writers' and Artists' Yearbook* indicate the date when they were founded – who may have more room for you on their list of clients. When going through the list, look at the same time not only for the agency's requirements (e.g. an enquiry letter first, before sending material), but also to see whether they handle only certain genres. Very few agents will deal with short stories or features for magazines and newspapers or poetry because their rewards, as a percentage of the payment, are not likely to be adequate for the considerable work which would be involved. Most agencies work with books of all kinds and in a number of different media, while some are specialists, handling only plays for the theatre, for example, or perhaps only children's books, and others, equally, may refuse to take on certain genres, such as children's books or science fiction.

However, if you are lucky enough to persuade an agent to take you on, there are many benefits. To begin with, the agent will submit your work to concerns which might be interested in it without charge to you. What is more, the publishers or managements to which it is sent are likely to pay far more attention to it than if you had submitted it directly. This is because they know that it has been through the sieve of consideration by the agency, which would not be handling it if it were without merit, and because they know that the agent is aware of what kind of material is of interest to them, and will not waste their time by sending in books of the sort that they do not want. Moreover, if the agent is clearly enthusiastic about the work, that enthusiasm can become infectious.

Once an offer for the work, or certain rights in it, is made, the agent will negotiate terms and endeavour to get the best possible deal for the author. This does not mean that the difference between an agented deal and one which you arrange yourself is likely to be of enormous significance, unless perhaps the agent believes that you have produced something in the bestseller class, or have come up with an idea which seems to have enormous potential. Submit such a proposal yourself and you may get a reasonably good deal, because the people who buy the rights to such properties are not normally in the business of cheating an author; but an agent's recognition of the proposal's value might push the purchaser into a much more generous contract and ensure that the book or play or whatever it is gets the treatment which it deserves.

However, with a modest book by an unknown author, an agent might be able to increase the advance from, say, £2000 to £2500, but would be unlikely to succeed in pushing it up as far as £10,000, or might arrange that the basic 10% royalty would go up to 12½% after the sale of 2500 copies, rather than the 5000 copies suggested by the publishers, but would not be able to persuade the publisher that the starting figure should be 12½%, or would be able to negotiate only a marginally better split of income from the sale of subsidiary rights. However, the moneys to be paid are not the only consideration; an additional reason for wanting to have an agent is that he or she will, in most cases, actually draw up the agreement or check the purchasers' contract for fairness.

It is normal for agents in this country to retain certain rights, such as United States and foreign-language rights, first serial rights and film rights, on behalf of the author, rather than granting them to publishers or any other purchaser of the main rights. The agent will then to try to sell these retained rights on the author's behalf, often using an associated agency. This does not mean that if you approach publishers or other purchasers directly, these rights will not be sold, because a purchasing company will try itself to sell them, but most agencies would claim that they are capable of achieving a better sale, simply because that is their main business, whereas it is a subsidiary matter for most purchasers.

Once a contract has been signed, moneys should become due to you. There will probably be an advance and, with luck, royalties will also be paid at some stage. It is the agent's job to collect those sums, to check the paperwork concerned, especially the royalty statements, making sure that all the percentages are correct. Most agents manage to complete this work and pass the relevant cheque to you within three weeks of receiving the money from publishers or management.

An additional and important function of the agent is to suggest new projects to the author-client and to obtain commissions for such projects and for the ideas put forward by the author, and to promote the author and his/her work to all those who might be interested in buying it. The success of major bestsellers, as has already been suggested, often begins with the agent's enthusiasm.

The personal relationship between the agent and the author is of major importance, because a good agent is not solely concerned with finding publishers or managements which will purchase the author's work, or obtaining commissions, nor just with negotiating contracts. In the first place, agents are often prepared to act as editors, suggesting changes to the work as it comes from the author before submitting it to potential purchasers, which is another reason why those who buy literary properties often prefer to do so from an agent rather than directly from the author, because not only can they expect a reasonable quality, but there is a good chance that the agent will have persuaded the author to iron out any glitches in the original version.

Authors often worry about whether they are being fairly treated by those who buy the rights in their work, and whether what happens, or does not happen, after the contract has been signed, is normal practice within the trade. One of the agent's most useful functions is to supply information and advice on such matters, to send their author-clients copies of all important documents and correspondence and, of course, to keep them up to date about the agency's activities on their behalf.

The agent will also chase up dilatory managements or publishers. Moreover, in the event of a dispute arising between the author and the purchaser of the work, it is the agent who will deal with the problem, fighting for the best possible outcome for the author, who, in the meantime, can remain on amicable terms with the person in the organisation with whom he/she usually deals.

Finally, and often most importantly, the agent is, or becomes, the author's friend – someone to whom it is possible to talk freely, to share concerns, a shoulder to cry on.

How honest and efficient are agents? They vary, like all human beings, but most will not cheat you and will work reasonably hard for you (since their own livelihood depends on your success). You may be reassured if you see that your agent is a member of the AAA – the Association of Authors' Agents – one of the functions of which is to set standards for the professional conduct of its members. However, you should not necessarily be put off using a new agency if it is not so shown, because a firm has to have been in existence for a certain period of time and to have a turnover of sufficient size before membership can be granted.

On the subject of agent's efficiency, one word of warning is needed: an agent will not go on working forever without seeing a return – in other words, if your work does not find a buyer within a comparatively short space of time, the agent will probably give up sending it out. The decision to abandon the work is not made solely on the basis of being unwilling to go on spending money on what appears to be a doubtful proposition (remember, agents themselves stand the costs of submitting books to potential customers). The agent very often knows that there is only a limited number of likely purchasers for the work in question; once they have all rejected it, the chances of a sale elsewhere are very poor. The acceptance of a new client by an agent means that the latter believes there is a likelihood of selling that author's work, but it does not mean that the agency's confidence in all the individual properties it handles is at the same level. If the agent is genuinely and personally enthusiastic about a certain property, he or she will probably go on trying to sell it for a much longer period than might otherwise be the case, but even then there will be a limit to the number of rejections before the agent gives up.

What do agents charge? Although a few agents ask for a fee before they will read a typescript, the majority indicate in the *Writers' and Artists' Yearbook* that they make no charge until the work has earned money (which usually comes in initially in the form of an advance paid on signature of contract). Up to that point they pay the expenses of submission, although you may be charged if the agent has to make photocopies, or use special messengers or send your typescript overseas, or purchase copies of your book from the publisher in order to send them to foreign publishers. Once your work generates payments, the basic fee is 10% or, quite frequently nowadays, 15%, of earnings in this country, but there is considerable variation in this matter, with some agencies charging considerably more. Fees on earnings from overseas, including the United States, usually work out at a minimum of 20%, because most agencies employ a sub-agent in foreign countries, and sub-agents take their cut before passing the money to the British agents, who then slice off their share.

If you find an agent it is usual nowadays to be asked to sign a contract. This will set out the basic agreement between you and the agent, and the terms, but it will also contain two important provisions.

The first is that you will place all your future work with the agent – apart from features for newspapers and magazines, short stories, single poems and any other short work, which agents are not usually interested in handling unless you are a very big name indeed, since their share of the income from each item is not large enough to justify the work involved. However, it is possible, if you so wish, to exclude certain genres of full-length work; and you might want to use a different agency for a specific kind of work, using, for example, one agent for your adult fiction and a different agent for your children's books. If you write for the stage, radio, television, and especially for films, you will almost certainly need a different agent from the one who handles your books.

Although many agents will deal with all kinds of literary work, most of them have certain 'no-go' areas, where they do not venture because they are not really competent to do a good job for their clients. It is not only a question of working in different media, such as films or television – if you write a book in a specialist area of fiction, such as fantasy sagas, you would probably be well advised to look for an agent who knows and likes the genre. Of course, if you are a client of one of the really big agencies, you will probably find that they have experts in every medium and genre, so different agents within the firm will handle different aspects of your work. Many smaller agencies (having secured your approval, of course) will pass the rights in your work which they do not feel capable of handling to an agent specialising in those rights, with whom they regularly share clients.

The second provision in agents' contracts with their authors is that if you leave the agent (normally after giving the period of notice defined in the agreement), the agent will continue to handle and take commission on all your works already placed by the agency.

Solicitors

When you first receive a contract in respect of a piece of literary work, you may be surprised at its length and complexity. How will you be able to tell if it is fair, or whether there are any nasty little things hidden away in the small print? Agents can be relied on to vet the agreement, but if you have gone directly to the purchaser of the material, to whom should you turn for expert advice?

Since the contract is a legal document, your first thought will probably be that you should consult a solicitor. Your own firm of solicitors is probably entirely reliable when it comes to conveyancing of houses or drawing up a will. If they also know something about the world of literature from a legal point of view, then you are going to be OK. It is far more likely, however, that they will not have that specialist knowledge and will not know which points in the contract are normal trade practice and which should be questioned. Indeed, you may receive entirely the wrong advice. You will then make a fuss about some things in the agreement which should be entirely acceptable and ignore others which should be fought tooth and nail.

Not surprisingly, there are solicitors who are very experienced in all matters concerning the various forms of literature and publication or performance, but unfortunately most of them reside in London, and are very expensive.

One of the best answers to the problem is to join the Society of Authors, or the Writers' Guild (see pages 109–12), either of which organisations will vet the contract for you.

At the very least you should consult other authors if you can (if you join your local writers' circle you will probably come across one or two published authors who will be willing to help) or some of the books available. My own book, *An Author's Guide to Publishing*, contains a sample of a Minimum Terms Agreement already discussed in Chapters 4 and 5. This is the form drawn up by the Society of Authors and the Writers' Guild in order to ensure that their members are fairly treated, not only in financial terms but in such matters as information and consultation.

It is not only in respect of a contract that you may need legal advice. If you quarrel with the purchaser of your work, or if either party claims that the other is in breach of the agreement, then you may need a solicitor. Sometimes the matter will go before a pair of adjudicators, one appointed from each side of the argument. For them trade experience is usually of more importance than a complete legal background. (Incidentally, if the arbitrators fail to agree on the issues about which they are asked to decide, the arrangement is usually that they then agree – usually an easier task – on a final adjudicator who will make a decision after hearing both sides of the matter.)

Sometimes, however, the case will come to court, and you will then certainly need expert advice from a solicitor and perhaps a barrister. It may well be worth going to one of the firms which specialise in literary matters, despite the expense. The level of expense provides a very powerful argument for joining either the Society of Authors or the Writers' Guild, since they will take on legal disputes, using their own solicitors, on behalf of their members. The only proviso is that you should be a member before the case arises – in other words, it is no use joining only when you are already in need of help and expecting them to take over.

Both the Society and the Guild will probably begin by advising you whether it is sensible to proceed with the case, or whether it would be better to give in or at least attempt to reach some compromise, so they will certainly not land you in more trouble unnecessarily. They can also help on occasion by suggesting someone who might act as your arbitrator, or as an expert witness in a case which is going to come to court.

Accountants, tax consultants and financial advisers

As has already been indicated in Chapter 7 with regard to Income Tax Returns, an accountant is far from being a luxury for anyone whose tax affairs are at all complicated and is essential if you are turning yourself into a limited company. You will, of course, want one who is highly competent in general terms and specifically able to deal with your particular financial affairs as an author. A suitable firm will not only prepare your company accounts and tax return in a form acceptable to the Inland Revenue, and on time, but will understand the way an author's income arises and is paid, and will know all the provisions of and amendments to the various Taxes Acts which apply to authors. Many very small accountancy firms, or indeed individuals, will meet those requirements, but unless you have special reasons for choosing such an outfit, it is probably wise to go to one of the larger firms, choosing one of those which specialise in looking after authors and artists and other 'abnormal' clients whose earnings are not taxed by means of P.A.Y.E., or at least one which has some other authors as clients. The Society of Authors, the Writers' Guild, the National Union of Journalists and other such organisations can provide a list of suitable firms. If you go elsewhere, find out what the charges will be and ask, before committing yourself, how many authors are already clients (of course, the accountants will not tell you who they are) and for how long.

If you are not setting up a limited company, you may decide to go to a tax consultant rather than an accountant. There's not much difference between them, in fact, and most tax consultants are quite capable of preparing year-end accounts, but their main function is advising you on your tax return and on what you can do, within the law, to avoid paying more tax than necessary, possibly by asking for an advance not to be paid until the following tax year.

Although many of us have a secret hankering for an adviser who know all the illicit loopholes and will be able to bend the tax laws on our behalf and save us lots of money, it is infinitely preferable to go to a firm which works strictly within the law. The shady accountant or tax consultant is likely to land you in trouble with the tax authorities, and he may fleece you into the bargain. In any case, one of the best arguments for using a straight-up firm, and this is particularly true of the larger companies, is that the Inland Revenue Inspectors know that they will not be presented with phoney accounts and claims – the firm will be too eager to preserve its reputation for that – and will, therefore, be much readier to accept the tax return without argument, and even to take a generous view of any claims.

Another helping hand could come from a financial adviser, especially if you become successful and have quite a lot of money in the bank. Accountants do not advise their clients what to do with their money, what investments to make or to sell, what ISA to buy, and so on, and indeed are forbidden by their professional associations to give such guidance. For assistance of that kind, you will need a financial adviser. Some of the larger firms can offer accountants, tax consultants and financial advisers under one roof, and this may simplify matters for you.

Associations for authors

1 Society of Authors
The Society of Authors was founded in 1884 by Walter Besant, and is the larger of the two associations for writers other than journalists (the other being The Writers' Guild of Great Britain – see below). It has more than 6000 members, having doubled in size in the last ten or twelve years, and is administered by a professional staff and a Management Committee consisting of elected members of the Society. It is officially an independent Trade Union, but it is not affiliated to the TUC and is strictly non-political.

To be eligible for full membership, a writer must have had a full-length work published or broadcast or performed commercially, or have an established reputation in another medium (for example, as a writer of short stories or as a translator) within the UK. In certain circumstances, authors of self-published books are accepted for membership. Associate membership is available to authors who have had a book accepted for publication but not yet published, or who have had occasional work published or broadcast or performed.

The Society represents authors in general terms in negotiations with the Publishers Association and with individual publishers, with the BBC and other bodies which use the work of authors; it also makes representations to MPs of all parties and to the Government on such matters as Public Lending Right, the necessity of keeping VAT off books, copyright and the effect on authors of EU directives or proposed legislation. It keeps in close touch with the Arts Councils, the Association of Authors' Agents, the British Council, the Institute of Translation and Interpreting, the Secretary of State for National Heritage, and also with other organisations for writers, such as the Writers' Guild of Great Britain and the National Union of Journalists. It is a member of the European Writers' Congress, the National Book Committee, the British Copyright Council and the International Confederation of Societies of Authors and Composers.

One of the Society's most important campaigns, undertaken in association with the Writers' Guild, has been to improve the terms and conditions specified in publishers' contracts. The Minimum Terms Agreement (MTA) is not signed by individual authors, but by the Society and the Guild on the one hand and a publishing firm on the other. It covers all authors who are members of the Society or the Guild in their dealings with the publisher concerned. The MTA lays down ground rules not only about the financial rewards to which an author should be entitled, but also about the author's right to consultation over the book's blurb, the cover or jacket design, the print quantity, the publicity and promotion plans, and so on. Several major publishing firms have signed an MTA, but its influence has extended beyond those who are signatories, and in recent years almost all publishers have been readier to respect authors' rights and to treat them more even-handedly than in the past. The Society and the Writers' Guild continue to negotiate with publishers who have not yet signed the agreement to persuade them to accept it. (Incidentally, the main arguments which reluctant publishers put forward to explain their failure to sign are, firstly, that the circumstances surrounding every book and its author are so different that any attempt to cover them in a single document is doomed to failure, and secondly, that there is no need for them to sign since they already give even better terms than the MTA suggests. The first argument does not hold water. As for the second – ho hum . . .

Within its membership, the Society of Authors has special Groups to cover special interests, comprising Broadcasting, Children's Writers and Illustrators, Educational Writers, Medical Writers; the Translators' Association is also a part of the Society, as are Authors North and The Society of Authors in Scotland set up for members living in those regions.

The Society administers a number of prizes for writers in various categories, including fiction, poetry, travel writing and broadcasting. Some £80,000 is given away annually to two dozen or more winners.

The Society provides many services for individual members, including advice about publishers, agents and other persons with whom an author might be negotiating, legal representation when required (especially in the case of broken contracts, unpaid royalties and fees, copyright infringement, etc.), and the clause-by-clause vetting of contracts.

A quarterly journal, *The Author*, containing much useful information and articles of general interest to authors, goes to all members, and the Society also publishes a number of Quick Guides, covering a variety of subjects, such as libel, income tax, permissions and your copyrights after your death.

Other benefits for members include automatic membership of ALCS (see pages 73–5), a pension fund, a contingency fund for those who are in financial difficulties, a medical insurance scheme and discounts on books and stationery. The Society also organises a number of meetings during the year, not all of which take place in London.

The annual membership subscription currently costs £70 (reduced to £65 if paid by direct debit). Further information is available from the Membership Secretary, the Society of Authors.

2 Writers' Guild of Great Britain

Originally formed in 1959 as the Screenwriters' Guild, by members of the Society of Authors who felt that they needed an organisation which would be devoted specifically to their interests, the addition to the membership of dramatists and authors of books resulted in the founding of the Writers' Guild of Great Britain, which, while still the specialist association for screenwriters, now covers all genres of freelance writing. In 1997 the Theatre Writers' Union amalgamated with the Guild. The Guild is a Trade Union affiliated to the TUC, but is a non-political organisation, which does not pay any political levy and has no involvement with any political party.

Like the Society of Authors, the Guild represents its members in general terms in making representations to MPs and to the Government concerning Public Lending Right, the necessity of keeping VAT off books, copyright and the effect on authors of EU directives or proposed legislation, etc. It also has close working relationships with Equity and the Musicians' Union, is a member of the International Affiliation of Writers' Guilds and plays an important part in the European Writers' Congress.

The Guild has national agreements, covering the terms and conditions to be offered to its members, with the BBC (for both radio and television) and ITV companies, with the British Film and Television Producers Association, and with the Producers' Alliance for Cinema and Television. It also has agreements protecting dramatists in their agreements with all theatrical managements, other than those concerning theatres in London's West End. And, as mentioned above, the Guild joined with the Society of Authors to produce the Minimum Terms Agreement, and continues its efforts to protect its book-writing members by inducing more publishers to sign.

The Guild offers its members legal advice, arranges frequent meetings for specialist groups within its membership and produces a bi-monthly magazine, *Writers' Newsletter*. It also offers a number of other benefits, including free and automatic membership of ALCS (see pages 73–5).

The basic requirement for membership is that the author shall have been paid at Guild rates under a written contract for one or more pieces of work. The annual subscription is currently £80 plus 1% of that part of an author's income earned from professional writing in the previous twelve months, up to a maximum of £930. Candidate membership is available at £35 per annum for those who have yet to receive a written contract for any of their work. Further information is available from The Writers' Guild of Great Britain.

3 National Union of Journalists

The NUJ has some 28,000 members, the majority of whom are full-time working journalists; others are employed in magazine and book publishing, information services and other allied trades. However, regular freelance contributors to newspapers and magazines may also join (something like a fifth of the total

112

membership comes into this category), and special sub-branches are devoted to their interests.

As might be expected in the case of a major trade union, much of the NUJ's work is concerned with matters relating to employment, rates of pay, dispute procedures and pensions. Unemployment benefit, grants to members in financial distress, certain bursaries and a variety of commercial benefits are available. The union has a Code of Conduct to which all members are required to subscribe. It publishes a bi-monthly magazine, *Journalist*.

For further information, and details of how to join the NUJ write to the Membership Manager, National Union of Journalists. To become a member you will have to be proposed and seconded by existing members, but there is apparently no difficulty in overcoming this hurdle if you do not know any members. Current rates of subscription: the NUJ does not expect its members to pay more than 1% of their gross taxable income (or ½% if the income is less than £12,000 p.a.), subject to a minimum of £42.33 p.a. The top rates vary according to the kind of work you do – for example, the maximum requirement from a journalist working for a provincial paper is £127 p.a., whereas one employed by a national paper may have to pay up to £228 p.a.

4 Chartered Institute of Journalists

Although the senior organisation of the profession, founded in 1884 and incorporated by Royal Charter in 1890, the IOJ (as it is usually known) is a much smaller organisation than the NUJ. Its membership is largely made up of freelance writers, and it has special sections for broadcasters, motoring correspondents, public relations practitioners and overseas members. It offers advice and support to its members, including funds for those needing financial assistance.

The annual subscription is related to earnings, with a maximum of £160, or £80 for trainees. Occasional contributors to the media may become Affiliate members, with a maximum subscription of £110. For further information write to the General Secretary, The Chartered Institute of Journalists.

Other organisations for writers

Apart from the most important societies and associations already described, it is worth remembering that the Society of Authors and the Writers' Guild both have specialised groups and societies within the main organisation. Additionally there are many independent associations covering more particular interests. The current edition of the *Writers' and Artists' Yearbook* has almost fifty pages of societies, associations and clubs, and gives details of their activities and (where appropriate) how to join. Even if you eliminate those which are devoted to artists, those located overseas and the many societies interested in only a single author (The Jane Austen Society, The Kipling Society, etc.), there is still something for virtually any author, ranging from the well-known Romantic Novelists' Association, Poetry Society, Society of Women Writers and Journalists, and Crime Writers' Association, to the more specialised Sports Writers' Association of Great Britain, British Guild of Beer Writers, International Association of Puzzle Writers, Guild of Agricultural Journalists, Association of British Science Writers, Guild of Food Writers, Children's Book Circle and Association of Christian Writers. For writers working for the audio and visual media, there is the Broadcasting Entertainment Cinematograph and Theatre Union, Writers Section, and the Radio Academy. All these societies thrive because anyone eligible to join any one of them can be sure of then being in contact with people with the same interests. And they all offer various degrees of information, help and advice to their members.

The list also includes the Regional Arts Boards, Book Trust, the British Council, the Society of Indexers, International PEN and many other organisations which are broader in scope, but of general interest to writers. Some of them may, in some cases, be able to offer considerable assistance.

Writers' conferences

Although large numbers of the men and women who go to writers' conferences are beginners and those who, although they have been writing for years, have had little success, many established authors are also regular attenders. The main lectures are given by such authors, and also by editors, agents, radio producers and the like, who can speak with real authority on their subjects. The courses, lectures and other activities available are normally conducted by established authors. This means that a great deal of useful knowledge is on tap – not only about how to write, but on practical matters such as market research, how to get an agent, what to look out for in a contract

114

and so on. The information available is so wide in scope and so freely given that not only the beginners, but often the already established authors, find it of immense value, and these conferences work so well, at least in part, because those who attend have the same interests in common and are willing to share their knowledge.

It is not all hard work and no play, and for many of those who attend, the conference offers not only an opportunity to learn, but a few days of holiday-making. The longer conferences usually offer outings to local places of interest, and some have sports facilities, or a hall where dancing is possible. And there is always the bar, because writing is a thirst-making activity, especially when you are talking about it for most of the day. A great many writers go to the same conference every year, and this results in the development of enduring friendships.

The principal conferences are:

The Writers' Summer School. The oldest established conference (it was held for the first time in 1949) takes place at Swanwick, Derbyshire, for a week in August every year. For details write to Mrs Brenda Courtie (address at end).

Writers' Holiday. A week-long conference held in Caerleon, South Wales. For details write to Mrs D. L. Anne Hobbs (address at end).

Southern Writers Conference, a weekend conference held at Chichester, West Sussex, in mid-June. For details write to Mrs Lucia White (address at end).

Annual Writers' Conference, a weekend conference held in Winchester in June. For details write to Mrs Barbara Large (address at end).

Scottish Association of Writers' Weekend Conference, a weekend conference held at Crieff, Perthshire, in April. For details write to Ms Anne Graham (address at end).

Scottish Association of Writers' Weekend Workshop, held at Pitlochry, Perthshire, in October. For details write to Ms Anne Trevorrow (address at end).

South East Writers Association Weekend, held in Essex in April. For details write to Mrs Marion Hough (address at end).

Writers' circles

As with conferences, the members of writers' circles often include experienced authors who can be of great help with practical advice to beginners.

A *Directory of Writers' Circles* is available from its compiler, Mrs Jill Dick (address at end).

Adult education

Further education classes in Creative Writing are very popular, and are run by most local authorities and/or under the auspices of the WEA. The standard of tuition varies, according to the qualifications of the tutors, but there is nearly always something to be gained from them. The classes usually take place once a week during term time.

Many private adult education schools also offer short residential courses in Creative Writing, usually lasting a weekend or a week, and some of these combine holidays abroad with the tuition. There are also the well-known Arvon courses (for which subsidies from the Regional Arts Boards are sometimes available), in which prominent authors work largely on a one-to-one basis with their students.

Correspondence schools

Would-be authors are lured to the correspondence courses offered by writing schools by the advertisements which promise them a return of their fees if they have not been successful, as a result of the tuition they will receive, within a given time. These schools do not have the best of reputations – one does not hear often of bestselling writers who attribute their success to what a writing school taught them and stories abound of how flimsy reasons have been found for not refunding fees to unsuccessful writers. Nevertheless, they do have their achievers and they are not constantly taken to court by disgruntled clients. Perhaps the contempt with which they are often regarded is the result of their inability to turn sow's ears into silk purses.

Their courses offer individual attention and an assiduous student can undoubtedly learn a great deal from them. It is probably a matter of temperament; if this method of instruction suits you, there is no doubt that you will benefit from it.

Publications for writers

1 Magazines

As already mentioned, the Society of Authors produces a quarterly magazine, *The Author*, members of the Writers' Guild of Great Britain receive the *Writers' Newsletter* every other month, and the National Union of Journalists publishes the bimonthly *The Journalist*. Most societies for authors have their own journal, such as the Poetry Society's *Poetry Review* and the Society of Women Writers and Journalists' *The Woman Journalist*.

A great many authors will be interested in a wide range of those magazines which are specifically aimed at writers, in part because of the information they give about markets, or the advice contained in articles on various writing techniques, and in part because they are seen as potential markets for articles, features and stories written by their readers. That includes many of those listed below (addresses can be found in the *Writers' and Artists' Yearbook*).

Writers News Monthly. News, including information about markets, competitions, articles.

Writing Magazine Bi-monthly. Articles (mostly how-to) on writing.

Young Writer Every four months. Aimed at writers under 18.

The Book Collector Quarterly.

Book and Magazine Collector Monthly.

The Bookseller Weekly. The principal journal of the publishing and bookselling trades.

Publishing News Weekly. Another magazine about the publishing and bookselling trades.

Books Ireland Monthly. About Irish books and writers, aimed at librarians, booksellers and readers.

The New Writer Ten issues a year. Connected with the Ian St James Awards, it contains short stories and articles about the written word.

Books Magazine Quarterly. Reviews, features, interviews with authors.

British Journalism Review Quarterly. Comment, criticism, review of media matters.

Carousel – The Guide to Children's Books Quarterly.

The Literary Review Monthly.

London Review of Books Bi-monthly.

The New Writer Features, short stories, articles on all aspects of the written word.

Scottish Book Collector Quarterly.

Screen International Weekly. News and features on the international film business.

Signal, Approaches to Children's Books Every four months.

The Stage Weekly. The journal of the theatre.

2 Books

Apart from the reference books which should be on a writer's bookshelf, the most important of which have been listed in Chapter 2, books for writers are mainly aimed at those who want to improve their writing and to get into print. Several publishers have specialised in this field, producing books on a number of different genres, most of which contain a generous amount of useful advice: leading the way is the excellent series from A & C Black, followed by the range from Allison & Busby, Elm Tree Books and Robert Hale. Many other publishers have brought out books about writing, including the magazine *Writers News*, which also runs a book club for its subscribers, making available a wide selection of all the relevant publications. It may be invidious to mention a single title, but many tutors of creative writing would agree that *Becoming a Writer* by Dorothea Brande, although written more than half a century ago, is of quite outstanding quality and should be on every writer's bookshelf.

In addition to books aimed primarily at the writer, publishers regularly produce a great many biographies and autobiographies of authors, dramatists, film-makers and others connected with the writing business, along with histories of publishing houses and similar books, all of which may be of interest and relevance to the practising author.

9. Self-Publishing and Vanity Publishing

Self-publishing

Until the last couple of decades of the twentieth century, to publish your own book yourself was very much frowned on. It suggested that your work was not good enough to persuade a commercial publisher to take it on, and also that you were rather vain. Most self-publishing was confined to small volumes of verse and autobiographies by people whose friends constantly told them, 'You've led such an interesting life – you really ought to write a book about it.'

The attitude towards self-publishing has changed radically since then, and it has become respectable. Quite how this has happened is a bit of a mystery – the public at large is not usually well informed about the world of publishing, but has somehow become aware that it is neither vanity nor the poor quality of the work which has driven the author to self-publish, but the fact that commercial publishers can no longer take on a book with what they believe to be a limited appeal (the question of whether their judgements in this respect are always accurate is neither here nor there).

Since the number of new books published in this country seems to increase year by year, you might think that it would be comparatively easy to squeeze your way into print with a reasonably well-written book but, of course, the enormous numbers of books which do get published means that they are all fighting for limited space in the bookshops and for the often drastically reduced resources of the libraries. Every year publishers turn down thousands of well-written, interesting books for which they cannot see a large enough sale in the present difficult market. A sale of no more than a few hundred copies is not economically viable. With each book that they bring out, publishers are looking not just to break even after paying for manufacture and the author's royalty, but to make a gross profit which will pay for their staff, their publicity, their costs of warehousing and despatch, and their general overheads, and finally to see a net profit. Publication of a book demands an investment of a minimum of £5000, with the risk, especially if the author is unknown, of losing most of it. Even books by established writers which are expected to be bestsellers can go wrong, and the investment in such titles may have been many times more than the minimum quoted above.

This, then, is why it is so difficult to get published. But individuals, with no overheads to worry about, can produce economically a small edition of their own works, especially if they are not expecting to make money on the venture and can face with equanimity the prospect of being out of pocket at the end of the day.

There are several ways of going about self-publishing. You can have your typescript duplicated; if you have a computer, you can run off several copies, possibly with colour illustrations on some sheets, and have the pages bound (one method gums them at the left-hand side, forming a spine to the book, or there are those plastic affairs the teeth of which fit into slots punched in the paper). Most jobbing printers and copyshops can bind the pages in these ways and, indeed, may have other variations to suggest. This is undoubtedly the cheapest way for a self-publisher to produce copies of a book. However, while it may be adequate if all you want to do is to have a few copies to circulate among your friends and relations, the result will not look like a book, will not be suitable for libraries and will not attract any members of the public.

There are several printers who specialise in short printing and binding runs for the self-publisher. Their advertisements are to be found in magazines for writers (see page 117) and many are listed in the *Writers' and Artists' Yearbook*. They are used to dealing with material ranging from nothing more than a simple handwritten manuscript, to a more sophisticated approach of camera-ready copy and all the necessary accompaniments.

In the former case, they will initially key the text on a computer. After a word count, they will suggest page size, typeface and size, and style of binding. They will also produce a jacket or cover design, and advise on such matters as ISBNs and the need to send copies of the book to the six Statutory Libraries. In the latter case, they probably have little to do other than to follow the author's instructions, but if you do not know how to prepare camera-ready copy (you will, of course, need to have a computer on which you can produce it), they will readily give advice. There are also several books available which will give you guidance.

The costs of producing the book will naturally vary according to the amount of work to be done by the printer, the length and page size of the book (most firms can cope equally well with a short book – perhaps 32 pages of poetry – or a much longer novel or autobiography), the style of the binding, the nature of the jacket, the number of illustrations, and so on, and particularly on the number of copies produced, since the price per copy becomes cheaper the more are printed and the origination costs (the charges for setting the book in type, preparing the jacket, etc.) are spread over the whole print run. Printers will quote for any quantity you want – the price if you are looking for ten or twelve copies only will be astronomic, but will appear much more reasonable if you want 50, 100 or 250 copies, or more. As well as quoting for the quantity you asked for, printers usually give a 'run-on' price for additional copies printed at the same time – for example, if you were to ask for 100 copies, you might also get a costing for 'per 25 copies run on'. It is very tempting when you see the figures to order the extra copies but, as explained later, you should be very wary of doing so.

It is, of course, quite impossible to give much idea of what the costs will be (except that, if you want to use full-colour illustrations, they will be horrendous), because books and the styles in which they are produced vary so much, but if, when you receive an estimate from a printer, the figures are higher than you had hoped, it may be possible to reduce them. Firstly, you should shop around – there can be quite a variation in the charges made by different concerns. Secondly, you would bring the costs down by producing camera-ready copy, for which you would need word-processing equipment with a good printer and good paper). Thirdly, you might consider reducing the typesize, cutting all or some of any illustrations (especially any intended to be in full colour), and using a simple two-colour jacket design, rather than a full-colour photograph. And the manufacturer may be able to suggest other economies in the production. Although you will naturally want to avoid cutting the costs to such an extent that the appearance of the book is badly affected, you may be able to save enough to make the proposition more attractive.

If you have any idea of selling copies of your self-published book, and trying to recoup some of your costs, it is advisable to obtain an ISBN (International Standard Book Number) for your book, which will enable booksellers and librarians throughout the world to identify it. If you manage to sell copies to Public Libraries, the ISBN will make it possible for you to register for PLR (see pages 71–4) on the book, which might be a small help towards recouping your costs.

To get an ISBN, for which there is no charge, you should apply to the Standard Book Numbering Agency, run in association with J. Whitaker & Sons Ltd; you will need to give the title of the book, the name of the author, the name and address of the publisher (you could call yourself more or less whatever you like – Joan Bloggs Press, perhaps, or Hollyhock Productions – but make sure if you can that the name is not already in use, which you can probably find out from a friendly bookseller or by checking with J. Whitaker). You should also send details of the book, when it is published, to Whitaker Bibliographic Services (telephone 020-7420 6000 for details about how to do this), which will mean that it is registered without charge on the lists which are available for booksellers and others in the trade.

Whether your book is published privately or more publicly, you have a legal obligation to send a free copy to The British Library, Copyright Receipt Office, and a further five free copies (for the Bodleian Library, Oxford, the Library of Cambridge University, the Library of Trinity College, Dublin, and the National Libraries of Scotland and Wales) to the Agent for the Libraries (address at end). Make sure that enclosed with the copy for the British Library is a note giving the list price of the book.

On the reverse of the title page of the book, various notices should be printed. These are: the title of the book, a statement on the lines of, 'First published in Great Britain 2001 by Hollyhock Productions' and the address of the publisher (presumably your own address), an assertion of your Moral Right of Paternity (see pages 40–1) and the manufacturer's imprint, which the printer and binder will supply. Although it is no longer necessary to include a copyright line, to insert one may serve as a warning to anyone who thinks, in its absence, that your work is not protected.

If you are hoping to sell copies of the book, you will also need to decide on its retail price. When you do so, bear in mind that any bookshops which sell copies will expect to take up to 50% of the proceeds. It is wise to calculate all your expenses, including any publicity which you are likely to pay for, divide the total by the number of copies you are producing, and then double that resulting figure to reach a retail price. If it does not seem excessive (look at similar books in bookshops), add on a little more. If you are hoping to recoup all your costs and to make a profit, add on a lot more. Incidentally, commercial publishers usually multiply the manufacturing costs per book by at least five to arrive at a published price, but of course they are likely to have a much lower production cost than you on a book which is similar to yours in length and style, because they will be able to print more copies than you would want to risk. Commercial publishers are also restricted to some extent by trade practices (for instance, novels are always priced lower than non-fiction of comparable length) and by the need to be competitive. Unless your costs forbid it, it is undoubtedly sensible to put a price on your book which is in the same range as those used by the mainstream publishers (other than the mass-market paperback houses, which keep their costs and prices down by producing large quantities of their books).

All this is fairly easy, and should not be excessively expensive, especially since you have some hope of recouping at least a part of your expenditure. The difficult part is in selling copies of the book – much more difficult than you may think. Of course, all your relations and friends will buy copies, won't they? That idea is all right in theory, but in practice they will probably expect to be given copies and, when you make it clear that you are not about to do that, they will borrow from each other. However, if you can be fairly hard-nosed about it and if you explain that you really can't afford to give *everybody* a copy, you may make quite a few sales. Since the price you have put on the book should be substantially larger than the cost, you may tempt your meaner friends by offering them a discount. But even then the sales figures are unlikely to be large.

You need to get the book into the bookshops and this is quite a difficult task. Commercial publishers employ a team of representatives, and still often fail to achieve a wide distribution of many of the books on their lists. For you to act as your own sales representative will be an extremely demanding undertaking in terms of both time and expense if you want to cover the entire country, and you are likely to find it very depressing into the bargain. Selling by telephone is a possibility but you will be extremely lucky to get very far. The best bet is with your local bookshops which you can visit in person. Choose the independents, who can make their own decisions, rather than branches of the big chains, which may have to refer to an unsympathetic head office before being allowed to place an order. Local bookshops will probably be willing to take a few copies on sale or return, meaning that they will keep the book on their shelves for a limited period, after which they will return the unsold copies to you (you will probably have to collect them yourself) and pay you for any copies they have sold. The more generous a discount you offer, the more willing they will be to take copies and the longer they will allow them shelf space.

It is certainly worth approaching Public Libraries to see if they are willing to buy copies of the book (write to the Chief County Librarian of the various counties, sending a sample copy). With any luck you should get a positive response at least from the county in which you live or in which the book is set. Unfortunately, however, Public Libraries do not usually have much spare cash for self-published novels by unknown authors and you are likely to have a better chance with non-fiction. If all else fails, it is worth presenting free copies to Public Libraries. Your book will then be read by members of the public who otherwise would not have heard of it, and there is always the chance that you will get some Public Lending Right money (provided, of course, that you remember to register the book – see pages 71–4).

You will, of course, help your cause if you can make a lot of people aware of the book's existence. Don't even think about inserting a display advertisement in a newspaper. It is likely to be a waste of money and even a small ad will probably not be very effective. On the other hand, if your book is of specialised interest, it would probably be worthwhile to insert an advertisement in any journal devoted to the particular subject. A better course of action than any direct form of advertising is to send review copies to any such magazine and to your local newspapers, especially if you can attach a 'news' story (*'I got through two thousand eight hundred and seventy-three cups of tea while writing my book,'* says local author.), but don't expect to get any notices in the national press.

It may also be worth your while to prepare a leaflet or flier and send it out to interested persons. This, too, tends to be much more effective for non-fiction than for fiction or poetry, because it is often possible to use the mailing list of an organisation which is interested in the subject of the book. Otherwise, it can be another time-consuming and expensive operation.

Another possibility, if you are on the Internet, is to make up your own website, with details about the book, a picture of the cover and information about its cost. Give your e-mail address so that potential customers can get in touch with you.

If you advertise your book in magazines or on a personal website, remember to add not only the address to which any orders should be sent, but the retail price on which you have decided, plus the cost of postage (probably at least £1, because that will also cover the cost of the Jiffy bag required). It may be worth your while, too, to include a dollar price and, if the book is likely to appeal to a non-English-speaking readership, the price in the appropriate currency. Remember that you will have to allow not only for greater mailing costs for overseas sales, but for the charge that your bank will make when buying foreign cash from you.

The difficulty in selling copies of a self-published book is the reason why you should be extremely cautious about the print quantity. Take a pessimistic view and, when you have calculated the number of copies that you are quite certain to be able to dispose of, cut that number too. If your book is a success, you can always order a small reprint, but unsold copies not only mean that you may lose quite a lot of money, but will give you a storage problem – books take up a lot of space.

It is well worth joining Author-Publisher Network (address at end), an organisation for self-publishers which can offer considerable assistance in the form of advice, courses and lectures, and a catalogue of members' publications.

Vanity publishing

In some cases self-publishers may be considered vain, but the books that they produce are not examples of vanity publishing, which is a technical trade term, applied to a specialised form of publication. It is in fact a scam.

Vanity publishers masquerade as ordinary commercial publishers, but work in a very different way. If you send your book to a vanity press you will receive a reply praising your work and offering to publish it, but suggesting that you should, if possible, visit the publishers' offices. There you will be told that, because publishing conditions are so difficult, the firm will not be able to go ahead unless you are prepared to make a small contribution towards the costs of production. The amount will vary according to the vanity publishers' assessment of your wealth, but even at its very lowest level is unlikely to be less than £3000 or £4000 for a short book (unless it is perhaps a collection of poems occupying not more than 32 pages), and considerably more for anything beyond, say, 50,000 words in length. The amount that you are asked to pay will not be simply a contribution towards the costs, but the entire sum, plus the publishers' profit, although this fact will not be revealed to you. The vanity publishers will tell you that you will soon recoup your money, because you will receive a royalty of 33% per cent, unlike what will be described as 'the miserly 10%' that regular publishers would pay. You will also learn that the press has an efficient sales team and that review copies will be sent to all the important papers and journals.

It all sounds most encouraging, even when it is explained that no royalties will be payable on the first four hundred copies printed, which will be used for reviews and other publicity purposes and from which you will be able to buy copies for your own use. For the books you buy you will usually pay 'trade terms', following the practice of regular publishers, which means a discount of somewhere between 25% and 35%. This is a bit rich, seeing that you have paid for the books already. Some vanity houses, however, require you to pay the full published price, which is even richer.

Alas, you will never see a penny back; there will be no reviews, because all the papers and magazines know the vanity houses and will have nothing to do with their products; and no sales will materialise through bookshops, for the same reason. In any case, only four hundred copies of the book will be printed, so no royalties will be payable. And you will also discover that ordinary commercial publishers would have given you at least six free copies of your book, whereas the vanity press is charging you for the books, the manufacture of which you have already paid for.

The book itself will usually be quite well produced, and might perhaps be considered a handsome volume. However, even the most luxurious production of a self-published book, printed on hand-made paper, bound in calfskin, with markers and gilt edges and marbled endpapers, would probably set you back far less than the vanity publishers' charge for a far less sumptuous edition, and you would have a genuine opportunity of recouping some of your expenditure through sales, as explained earlier.

If this information about vanity publishers is new to you, you may well be asking whether such practices can be legal. Although news has just come through, as I write, of a successful prosecution against a vanity press for misleading an author and failing in its commitments, it is usually impossible to sue successfully, because their contracts are watertight legal documents. There is never anything in writing committing the publishers to anything which they do not do; and their oral communications are always carefully phrased so that, even if you tape-record your conversations, you will never catch them out. In other words, although you will have been wilfully misled, it will be by omission of information, rather than by anything which you can pin down. The one hope, again as I write, lies in the Government's intention to bring in a law designed to make the activities of 'rogue traders' illegal. This may be of some help, but is intended mainly to stop the 'cowboys' in the building trades, and it may not be worded specifically enough to catch the more sophisticated, legally well-advised proprietors of the vanity presses.

Unless you have more money than you know what to do with, never go near the vanity publishers. Of course, the choice is yours, and you may feel that the extra cost is worth it because of the ease of the whole operation as far as you are concerned. All you have to do is to write the book and then write a cheque. Admittedly, self-publishing involves a great deal more hassle for you (preparing the copy, hunting around for a printer, making decisions about what the book will look like, storing it and trying to sell it, etc.), but you will be paying the vanity publishers through the nose, and I would suggest that you should remind yourself of the old adage about fools and their money. If you do decide to ignore the good advice given in this section, then at least commit yourself to vanity publishers with your eyes open, knowing what to expect.

It is easy to recognise the vanity publishers: they are the ones who insert advertisements with some such wording as 'Authors Wanted' or 'Want to Get Into Print?'; regular commercial publishers don't need to do that, their problem being how to cope with the thousands of unsolicited typescripts that arrive without their asking for them.

10. The Professional Author

Understanding the business

Authors are rarely entirely happy with the manner in which those who purchase their work present or exploit it. Even if they are among the handful of extremely successful writers for whom everything possible is done to please and to maximise sales, such fortunate beings will probably have a grumble or two. The discontent is particularly strong when directed against book publishers. It is not surprising that there should be a certain amount of discontent. Looking, for example, at the authors on the one hand and the publishers on the other, you will see a difference of attitude towards a book which does less well than expected: an author will be thinking sadly of the time and effort that went into writing it, the unfulfilled hope of recognition, fame and fortune that it carries, and the incompetence of the publishers; publishers will be disappointed, too, but will remember that the book is just one of many that the firm will publish that year - indeed, one of the hundred thousand books which will be published in the UK in a twelve months' period – and some books sell well, and a larger number sell less well, and that's the way the cookie crumbles.

Authors also have other dissatisfactions. Despite the consultation which may take place if the publishers have signed or at least accepted some of the provisions of the Minimum Terms Agreement, publishers persist in giving books unattractive jacket or cover designs which have nothing at all to do with the book's contents, they publish at what is patently the wrong time of the year and, worst of all, they lose all interest in the book within a few months of its publication and make no effort thereafter to keep the sales moving. No wonder the book hasn't sold!

There are scores of complaints of this nature which almost all authors make. Are they justified? Sometimes but not by any means always, and authors tend to forget that publishers are as eager as they are to be successful with their books. After all, they have invested a considerable sum of money in each and every book which they publish, and they want not only to recoup that money but, as often as possible, to make a profit, without which the firm will not survive. Besides, the more successful the publishers are, the better the firm's chances of attracting more saleable authors to the list.

One of the problems in author/publisher relationships is that very few authors have much understanding of how publishers work, what the pressures are, what the reasons for failure may be, and which of an author's complaints are justified and which are not. An agent, if the author has one, should be able to explain matters; indeed one of the major advantages of having an agent is the ability to tell the author why this or that is happening or not happening and whether the issue should be raised with the publisher. The Society of Authors, the Writers' Guild and the other organisations for writers can also give useful advice, and so can your author friends. But even if you have an agent, and belong to all the right societies, and have friends who can help, it seems to me important that authors should themselves have some understanding of what publishers in general do or don't do, and why. And if you have no-one to advise you, it is even more important. It is part of being a professional. In any calling, professionals need to have a reasonably deep knowledge of what those they deal with do, and what the demands of the job and its difficulties are. This is particularly true of an industry as complex as publishing.

What can you do about this? Your publishers will either be unwilling to burden you with information about the inner workings of the firm (especially since some of the details may not be to its credit), or will tell you a long tale of woe, which will not inspire your confidence, or give you a whole string of barely credible assurances that everything will be absolutely perfect (and if it isn't, it isn't their fault anyway). What can you believe? The best thing is to try to get an overall view of the publishing business. For a start, read *The Truth About Publishing* by Stanley Unwin (now out of print, but still available in libraries); although dated, it gives a clear picture of how publishers go about their business. Secondly, read my own book, *An Author's Guide to Publishing*; and in case you think that I am merely trying to boost its sales, let me say, immodestly, that it is widely accepted as the most comprehensive and authoritative book on the subject.

This matter of understanding the business of those you deal with naturally applies in the same way if you are writing for radio or television, the stage, films, or for newspapers and magazines.

Contracts

Because a writer is an individual and the creation of a book is often a rather strange, unpredictable process, some authors are sometimes inclined to look upon the clauses of a contract as no more than a rough guide to various aspects of the work, subject to alteration according to the author's whims and temperamental moods. And if you don't believe me, ask any publishers – they all know authors like that. It is, of course, a highly unprofessional attitude. Although few of such authors would talk openly of their Muse, they have at the back of their minds the idea that writing is something that you do when you are inspired, and that if inspiration doesn't come, then you don't write. Professionals understand that writing is a job like any other, a job which has to be done whether you are in the mood or not. So they take seriously the clause in the contract which calls upon them to deliver a typescript at such and such a date, and they deliver what has been asked for – not something which 'popped into my mind and seemed much better', or a book twice as long as planned, or half the length. Indeed, they stick carefully to all the terms of the agreement which place a responsibility upon them – the clauses concerning delivery of the finished material, the warranty, the prompt return of proofs, etc.

So what do you do if, part way through writing whatever it may be, you want to change the work so that it differs from the synopsis on the basis of which the work was commissioned? What do you do if you realise that you are going to be late in delivering the finished work? What do you do if you need help in some matter which concerns the work? You telephone or write to the person who commissioned the work and tell whoever it may be about your problem. It makes sense, it is only polite, and there's a lot of truth in the old saying, 'a trouble shared is a trouble halved'.

Ethics

There are some things that you shouldn't do. It is part of being professional to be honest and fair to those with whom you deal. Consequently, you do not plagiarise or indulge in any other

130

form of literary stealing. If you write to anyone asking for information or help of some kind, you always include a stamped addressed envelope for the reply. If you employ an agent, you do not attempt to sell your work yourself. You do not put on airs and graces.

Of course, this is all Mrs Do-As-You-Would-Be-Done-By talk, and there may be occasions when it is justified to become Mrs Do-Unto-Others-As-They-Do-Unto-You. But on the whole (and please forgive the moralising), if you behave well towards others, they will behave well towards you, and are then deserving of your loyalty. Stay with the same agent, stay with the same management, stay with the same publishers, as long as they serve you reasonably well. Authors who constantly move around from one publishing firm to another, working with a succession of agents, always seeking the Big Time, and always being disappointed, should perhaps ask themselves whether it might possibly be the quality of their work which is restricting them.

Mind you, if you become a famous writer, you will undoubtedly be wooed by other publishers and agents and managements – by anyone who can smell big money – and it will be easy to forget loyalty and to leave those who have served you well. Go where the dollars are – probably to one of the conglomerates, because they have the money – if that is important to you. And why not? Only because you may find that you have swapped a publishing firm where you and the staff regarded each other as friends and in which both sides knew how the other one worked, for one where building a personal relationship has to start from scratch, and where, since it is probably a large company, everything is more than a little impersonal. You will have changed yourself from a writer into a money-making machine.

Accepting criticism

From time to time arguments arise about the activities of editors and especially copy editors. This is something which seems to apply almost exclusively to books. Newspapers and magazines edit work submitted to them, and those who write the material seem reasonably happy that they should do so. The director's word (and sometimes the actor's) seems to bear far more weight than the author's in the world of stage plays, radio, television and films. But with books a great many authors get grand ideas and resent the suggestions for improvement that come from editors.

Have you noticed how many writers, when they reach the top of the profession, become prolix? In their early days they would have taken the advice of their editors and cut and cut and cut. The sparer the prose, the stronger the writing becomes. Nowadays, however, let an editor suggest so much as the deletion of a comma, and the big-name author is off round the corner to publishers who won't want to change anything. It seems to me a very unprofessional attitude.

Admittedly one hears stories about stupid changes which have been made, usually as a result of ignorance but, on the whole, the professional author listens with gratitude to the points that editors make, knowing that their object is rarely if ever self-aggrandisement but the production of a better book. It is virtually impossible for authors to look at their finished work with complete detachment, and another pair of constructively helpful eyes should always be welcome.

Keeping records

Are you an organised person? Do you keep copies of all the work that you do, all the professional letters that you write? Do you file them, if not every day, at least frequently enough that you can always put your hand on the papers you need? Do you log your submissions so that you know what work is out, who has rejected it, who is still considering it, who has not yet seen it? As I have said before, being a professional writer is a business, and it needs to be conducted in a businesslike way.

Revision

Professionals revise their work as many time as necessary until it is as near perfect as they can make it. Amateurs don't.

Publicity

In surveys conducted by the Society of Authors to check their members' satisfaction or dissatisfaction with their publishers, the most consistently and vigorously raised complaint was of poor publicity and promotion. The reason usually is a lack of money, rather than any unwillingness on the publishers' part to tell the public about the firm's wares. In most publishing houses a budget sets the amount of money which can be spent on publicity and promotion for the whole list over a given period of time. Naturally, a big chunk of it goes to the books for which the publisher expects major sales, and what is left has to be shared out among all the other titles.

It is very difficult for authors to accept the truth that books are not all born equal, that some are going to be pushed out into the hard commercial world to make their way without the backing of a huge advertising campaign (or even a small one), and that some are going to die very quickly.

If you are dissatisfied with what is done for your book in the way of publicity and promotion, there is one thing that you can do to help and that is to take every opportunity which is offered to do your own publicity. Do it without shame. Discard your British shyness and tell people about your work, and how good it is. Trade on the fact that, to the public at large, authors have a certain glamour (goodness knows why!). And if it is available always have copies of your work to hand which you can sell to anyone interested. Don't ever give them away. That wouldn't be very professional.

Making a will

It is very important for everyone to make a Will, but especially for writers. If you can possibly afford it, go to a solicitor for help in drawing up the Will; otherwise at least buy a Will form, fill it up as best you can and get it witnessed. That will save those who have to sort out your affairs a lot of hassle. You can, of course, leave your money, your investments and your goods and chattels to a single legatee or to as many persons you wish, but it is worth remembering that gifts to a spouse are not subject to Inheritance Tax, nor are gifts to recognised charities.

The importance for a writer in making a Will is that among the assets which you will be leaving behind are your literary properties, which could be extremely valuable. When you make the Will you should consider what you want to happen to them and to any income that may accrue from them. This applies to both published and unpublished works, since your copyrights endure after your death, as explained in Chapter 4 (see page 35). The actual manuscripts (which term includes typescripts and material recorded on disc) are quite separate from the copyright and, like any other goods and chattels, can be bequeathed in any way you wish, without being tied to the copyright. You could, for instance, leave your copyrights to your partner and the manuscripts to a local museum (if, presumably, you think the museum would welcome them). However, in the case of unpublished work, which might be published after your death, it could cause complications to leave the two parts of the material to different legatees.

As with anything else that you own, if your copyrights or manuscripts are not specifically mentioned in your Will, they will become part of your residuary estate (that is, everything which is left after any specific bequests). If you are, or become during your lifetime, a famous author, it is obvious that your works could be extremely valuable to your legatees, but if you haven't had any such success, don't think that it is not worth bothering about these literary assets – there are many examples of authors who have become successful only after their death, but still within the period of copyright.

It's not a bad idea to include a statement of your wish that any typescripts or discs containing your work should not be destroyed. Even if the work has little chance of being commercially exploited, your family will be interested to see it.

For purposes of probate, again like any other of your assets, the value of the copyrights will be included in the estate. If they are already producing income in the form of royalties from publishers or performance fees, or are expected to do so, then a value will have to be placed on them. Negotiations will have to be entered into with the Capital Taxes Office, which will inevitably seek to assess the copyrights at the highest possible level, but will usually compromise with a valuation equal to two or three years' past average income. Obviously, circumstances vary, according to what property is left and what its earning power is expected to be. The negotiations are likely to be very difficult for the executors unless they are familiar with the writing business, but help may often be found from literary agents and the firms which used the deceased author's material..

In certain cases, it is possible to obtain 'business property relief' on the copyrights, and this loophole may be very useful if your estate will be in excess of the sum exempted from Inheritance Tax (currently £223,000), and if the income after your death which derives from your writing is likely to be significant (although gifts to a spouse, including the benefit of copyrights, are exempt from this tax). Further details on this score should be available from your solicitor.

Some successful authors, wanting to save their families from problems, appoint a 'literary executor'. Such a person would be familiar with the businesses likely to be involved, and might be a fellow author or – the obvious choice – the author's agent, if he or she has one. The function of the literary executor might be simply advisory, or could be the complete management, on behalf of the copyright owners, of all the testator's literary assets. A solicitor would advise on the necessary wording of the Will, which would probably specify that if the literary executor were to become the manager of all the copyrights, it would be 'in trust' for those named in the Will as owners of the copyrights. If you simply want your existing agent to continue to carry out an agent's normal functions after your death, you do not need to appoint him or her as a literary executor, but it is certainly worth including a statement in the Will indicating that you wish your legatees to continue to employ the agent in the normal way.

And finally . . .

If you are a genius, and manage to get recognised as such, you needn't bother yourself with any of the information and advice in this book. All you need to do is to go on writing. And you will be able to afford to pay others to look after the nuts and bolts. But for most of us, it's a hard world that we live in, and the environment is not one in which you can get very far as an airy-fairy dreamer, interested only in your Art. It pays to be professional. The people you work with, who take what you have written and present it to the public in whatever form it may be, always prefer to deal with writers who are businesslike and have their feet on the ground. It is to help you to become fully professional in your approach that this book has been written.

Addresses

Agent for the Libraries (the five, apart from the British Library, that receive free copies), 100 Euston Street, London NW1 2HQ

Association of Authors' Agents (AAA), 62 Grafton Way, London W1P 5LD, tel: 020 7387 2076, fax: 020 7387 2042

Association of Learned and Professional Society Publishers, South House, The Street, Clapham, Worthing, West Sussex BN13 3UU, tel: 01903 871686, fax: 01903 871286, e-mail: alpsp@morrisassocs.demon.co.uk, website: www.alpsp.org

Author-Publisher Network, 6 Kelvinbrook, West Molesey, Surrey KT8 1RZ

British Film and Television Producers' Association, c/o PACT

British Library, Legal Deposit Office, Boston Spa, Wetherby, West Yorkshire LS23 7BY, tel: 01937 546000, website: portico.bl.uk

Copyright Licensing Agency (CLA), 90 Tottenham Court Road, London W1P 0LP, tel: 020 7631 5555, fax: 020 7631 5500, e-mail: cla@cla.co.uk, website: http://www.cla.co.uk

Directors' Guild, The, 15–19 Great Titchfield Street, London W1P 7FB, tel: 020 7436 8626, fax: 020 7436 8646, e-mail: guildedggb.co.uk, website: www.dggb.co.uk

Periodical Publishers' Association, Queens House, 28 Kingsway, London WC2B 6JR, tel: 020 7404 4166, fax: 020 7404 4167, e-mail: info1@ppa.co.uk, website: http://www.ppa.co.uk

Producers' Alliance of Cinema and Television (PACT), 45 Mortimer Street, London W1N 7TD, tel: 020 7331 6000, fax: 020 7331 6700

Public Lending Right Office (PLR), Richard House, Sorbonne Close, Stockton-on-Tees, Cleveland TS17 6DA

Publishers' Association (PA), 1 Kingsway, London WC2B 6XF, tel: 020 7565 7474, fax: 020 7836 4543, e-mail: mail@publishers.org.uk

Publishers' Licensing Society (PLS), 5 Dryden Street, London WC2E 9NW, tel: 020 7829 8486, fax: 020 7829 8488

Scottish Independent Radio Producers Association, c/o Forsyth Productions, 52 Granby Road, Edinburgh EH16 5PZ, tel: 0131 667 9573

Society of Indexers, Globe Centre, Penistone Road, Sheffield SA6 3AE, tel: 0114 281 3060

Standard Book Numbering Agency/J. Whitaker & Sons Ltd,
12 Dyott Street, London WC1A 1DF

Whitaker Bibliographic Services, tel: 020 7420 6000

Organisations for writers

Alliance for the Protection of Copyright, c/o BECTU

Authors' Foundation, c/o The Society of Authors

Authors North, c/o The Society of Authors

Authors' Licensing and Collecting Society (ALCS), Marlborough
Court, 14–18 Holborn, London EC1N 2LE, tel: 020 7395 0600,
fax: 020 7395 0660, e-mail: alcs@alcs.co.uk, website: www.alcs.co.uk

British Association of Journalists, 88 Fleet Street, EC4Y 1PJ, tel: 020
7353 3003, fax: 020 7353 2310

Broadcasting Entertainment Cinematograph and Theatre Union
(BECTU), 111 Wardour Street, London W1V 4AY, tel: 020 7437
8506, fax: 020 7437 8268, e-mail: info@bectu.org.uk, website:
www.bectu.org.uk

Chartered Institute of Journalists (IOJ), The, 2 Dock Offices, Surrey
Quays Road, London SE16 2XU, tel: 020 7252 1187, fax: 020 7232
2302, e-mail: cioj@dircon.co.uk

Freelance Consortium, The, c/o BECTU

Institute of Translation and Interpreting (ITI), 377 City Road,
London EC1V 1NA, tel: 020 7713 7600, fax: 020 7713 7650,
e-mail: info@iti.org.uk, website: http://www.iti.org.uk

National Union of Journalists (NUJ), Acorn House, 314–320 Gray's
Inn Road, London WC1X 8DP, tel: 020 7278 7916, fax: 020 7837
8143, e-mail: nuj@mcr1.poptel.org.uk

Poetry Society, 22 Betterton Street, London WC2H 9BU, tel: 020
7420 9880, fax: 020 7240 4818, e-mail: poetrysoc@dial.pipex.com,
website: http://www.poetrysoc.com

Royal Literary Fund, 3 Johnson's Court, off Fleet Street, London
EC4A 3EA, tel: 020 7353 7150, fax: 020 7353 1350

Scottish Association of Writers, c/o Ms Anne Graham, 55 Grange
Loan, Edinburgh EH9 2ER

Society of Authors, The, 84 Drayton Gardens, London SW10 9SB,
tel: 020 7373 6642, fax: 020 7373 5768, e-mail:
authorsoc@writers.org.uk, website: www.writers.org.uk/society

Society of Authors in Scotland, The, Bonnyton House, Arbilot, Angus DD11 2PY, tel: 01241 874131, fax: 01241 874131, e-mail: eileen@ramsaye.freeserve.co.uk

Society of Women Writers and Journalists (SWWJ), 110 Whitehall Road, London E4 6DW, tel: 020 8529 0886

Women in Film and Television, 6 Langley Street, London WC2H 9JA, tel: 020 7240 4875, fax: 020 7379 1625, e-mail: info@wftv.org.uk, website: www.wftv.org.uk

Workers' Educational Association (WEA), National Office, Temple House, 17 Victoria Park Square, London E2 9PB, tel: 020 8983 1515, fax: 020 8983 4840, e-mail: info@wea.org.uk, website: www.wea.org.uk

Writers' Guild of Great Britain, The, 430 Edgware Road, London W2 1EH, tel: 020 7723 8074, fax: 020 7706 2413, e-mail: postie@wggb.demon.co.uk, website: www.writers.org.uk/guild

Details for many more organisations for writers may be found in the *Writers' and Artists' Yearbook*

Writers' groups
Directory of Writers' Circles – write to: Mrs Jill Dick, Oldacre, Horderns Park Road, Chapel-en-le-Frith, High Peak SK23 9SY

Annual Writers' Conference, Winchester – write to: Mrs Barbara Large, Chinook, Southdown Road, Shawford, Hampshire SO21 2BY

Scottish Association of Writers' Weekend Conference, Crieff – write to: Ms Anne Graham, 55 Grange Loan, Edinburgh, EH9 2ER

Scottish Association of Writers' Weekend Workshop, Pitlochry – write to: Ms Anne Trevorrow, Old Quarterhouse, Darvel, Ayrshire KA17 0ND

South East Writers Association Weekend, Essex – write to: Mrs Marion Hough, 47 Sunningdale Avenue, Leigh-on-Sea, Essex SS9 1JY

Southern Writers Conference, Chichester – write to: Mrs Lucia White, Stable House, Home Farm, Coldharbour Lane, Dorking, Surrey RH4 3JG

Writers' Holiday, Caerleon – write to: Mrs D. L. Anne Hobbs, 30 Pant Road, Newport NP9 5PR

Writers' Summer School, Swanwick – write to: Mrs Brenda Courtie, The Rectory, Blisworth, Northants NN7 3BZ

Index

140